W9-BNR-438

PRINCE EDWARD ISLAND

ANDREW HEMPSTEAD

Contents

Charlottetown and Queens County

A

s Canada's smallest provincial capital, Charlottetown (pop. 35,000)—the island's governmental, economical, cultural, and shopping center—makes no pretense of being a big city. Rather, this attractive town is walkable, comfortable, and friendly. Its major attractions include a beautiful harborside location, handsome public and residential architecture, sophisticated art and cultural happenings, and plentiful lodgings and appealing restaurants.

The city also makes a good sightseeing base for exploring surrounding Queens County, which is the definitive Prince Edward Island as you imagined the province would be. The region is temptingly photogenic, a meld of small seaports with brightly colored craft at anchor and farmland settings with limpid ponds and weathered barns. Along the Gulf of St. Lawrence is Cavendish, the island's most popular tourist destination. Cavendish was the childhood home of Lucy Maud Montgomery, who created perfection on earth within the pages of her books, which centered on the spunky heroine Anne of Green Gables.

HISTORY

In the late 1750s, English surveyor Samuel Holland surveyed all of Prince Edward Island, recommending that the main settlement be established on a peninsula within Hillsborough Bay. He named it Charlotte, for the consort of King George III. The town had its grid laid out in 1764 and was named the island's capital the next year. Charlottetown's development paralleled the island's development. A road network was laid out by 1850. And by 1860, some 176 sawmills were transforming forests into lumber, greasing the island's economy and providing the raw materials for a thriving shipbuilding industry. As the center of government and commerce, the town was enriched with splendid stone churches and public buildings, many of which date to the mid-1800s and stand to this day.

Previous: lighthouse in Borden-Carleton; Peake's Wharf. **Above:** the lighthouse at North Rustico Harbour.

Look for ★ to find recommended sights, activities, dining, and lodging.

Highlights

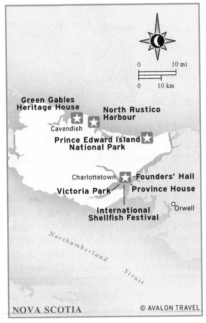

★ **Province House:** This historic sandstone building in the heart of Charlottetown hosted the Fathers of Confederation in 1864 and continues today as the provincial seat of government (page 9).

★ **Victoria Park:** Take a break from the relative bustle of downtown with a walk through this waterfront park, home to the impressive Fanningbank residence (page 13).

★ **International Shellfish Festival:** You can feast on seafood year-round in Charlottetown, but this late-September festival is the place to try all your favorites at once (page 15).

★ **Prince Edward Island National Park:** Stretching along the Gulf of St. Lawrence, this park is one of the island's few undeveloped tracts of land. Warm water, beaches, and red cliffs are the main draws (page 26).

★ **North Rustico Harbour:** It's just a dot on the map, but this small fishing village is particularly photogenic. A lighthouse, kayak tours, and an excellent restaurant add to the appeal (page 30).

★ **Green Gables Heritage Place:** Northern Queens County is lovingly known as "Anne's Land," for Anne of Green Gables, one of the world's best-known literary characters (page 32).

★ **Founders' Hall:** Canadians especially will enjoy learning about how the Dominion of Canada was created at this harbor-front interpretive center (page 9).

Charlottetown and Queens County

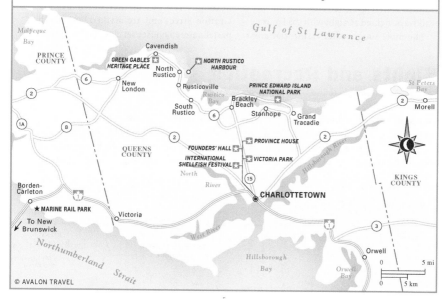

PLANNING YOUR TIME

For many visitors, Queens County *is* Prince Edward Island. A typical itinerary would be to catch the ferry to Wood Islands, spend one day in the capital, Charlottetown, and another in Cavendish before driving off the island via the Confederation Bridge. This is enough time in the capital to visit major attractions such as **Founders' Hall** and **Province House** while having enough time to end the day with an evening walk through **Victoria Park.** If your travels coincide with the late September **International Shellfish Festival,** you may want to stay longer.

Cavendish, the most popular destination on all of Prince Edward Island, is just an hour's drive from the capital. This makes a day trip possible and means you can settle yourself into Charlottetown for two or more nights, taking advantage of the theater and many restaurants. Cavendish does have many accommodations, but good dining rooms are severely lacking. Regardless of where you stay, your trip to Cavendish should include a drive through **Prince Edward Island National Park,** the short detour to **North Rustico Harbour,** and a visit to **Green Gables Heritage Place.**

ORIENTATION

The city, small as it is, may be baffling for a new visitor because of the way historic and newer streets converge. The town began with a handful of harbor-front blocks. The centuries have contributed a confusing jumble of other roads that feed into the historic area from all sorts of angles.

From either direction, the **TransCanada Highway** (Route 1) will take you right into the heart of town. From the west, it crosses the North River, turns south at the University of Prince Edward Island campus, and becomes University Avenue. From the east, take the Water Street exit to reach the information center.

Extending from the harbor to Euston Street, the commercial area is pleasantly compact, attractive, and easily covered on foot. **Old**

Charlottetown (or Old Charlotte Town, depending on who's describing the area) has been restored with rejuvenated buildings and brick walkways, lighted at night with gas lamps.

The most sought-after residential areas, with large stately houses, rim Victoria Park and North River Road. Working-class neighborhoods fan out farther north beyond Grafton Street and are marked with small pastel-painted houses set close to the streets.

Sights and Recreation

Downtown Charlottetown is compact; plan on parking and exploring on foot. The waterfront area is the best place to leave your vehicle. Not only is it central, but you can make the provincial **Visitor Information Centre** (6 Prince St., 902/368-4444, www.discover-charlottetown.com; May daily 9am-5pm, June daily 9am-6pm, July-Aug. daily 8:30am-6pm,

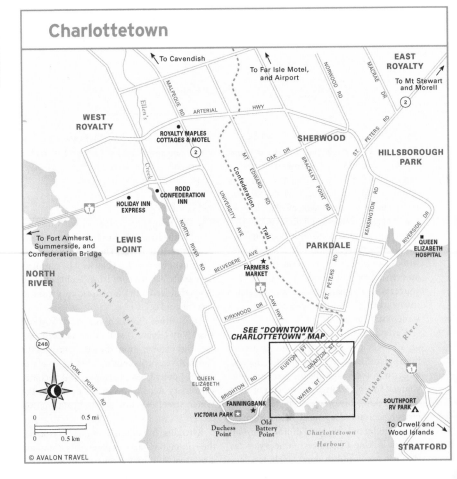

Charlottetown

© AVALON TRAVEL

Sept. daily 8:30am-5pm, Oct. daily 9am-4pm) your first stop.

DOWNTOWN
★ Founders' Hall

Years of restoration saw a historic railway building transformed into Founders' Hall (6 Prince St., 902/368-1864; 6 Prince St., 902/368-4444; May daily 9am-5pm, June daily 8:30am-6pm, July-Aug. daily 8:30am-7pm, Sept. daily 8:30am-5pm, Oct. daily 9am-4pm; adult $9.50, senior $8.50, child $6.25), Charlottetown's number-one attraction. Located on the harbor beside the information center, this state-of-the-art facility combines the latest technology, dynamic audiovisuals, holo-visuals, and interactive displays to create a very different museum experience. You'll enter the Time Tunnel and travel back to 1864, when the Fathers of Confederation first met to discuss the union of Canada. You'll proceed through history, from the formation of each province and territory to modern times.

Confederation Players

The Confederation Players are keen local historians who dress in period costume to conduct walking tours ($12.50 pp) of downtown Charlottetown from Founders' Hall mid-June through August. The regular one-hour tour departs daily at 11am; a one-hour tour for French speakers departs at 3pm; and the Ghostly Realm Tour departs Monday-Saturday at 7:30pm.

Downtown Waterfront

A rejuvenation project has seen much improvement in the downtown waterfront precinct, much of it spurred on by the establishment of Founders' Hall. The adjacent Confederation Landing Park is rimmed by a seaside boardwalk and filled with pleasant gardens and well-trimmed grass. The park is integrated with Peake's Wharf, where the Fathers of Confederation arrived on the island. This is now a tourist hub of sorts, with restaurants and shops, and tour boats line the docks waiting to take interested visitors on sightseeing trips.

★ Province House

The nation of Canada began at Province

Founders' Hall

Downtown Charlottetown

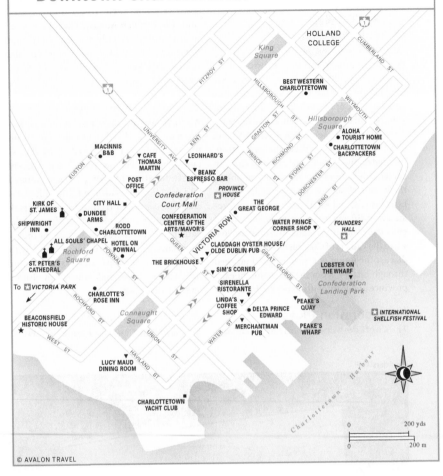

© AVALON TRAVEL

House (corner of Grafton St. and Great George St., 902/566-7626; June-Sept. daily 9am-5pm, Oct.-May Mon.-Fri. 9am-5pm; free), four blocks up Great George Street from the harbor. Now protected as a national historic site, the buff sandstone neoclassical edifice at the high point of downtown was erected in 1847 to house the island's colonial legislature. It quickly became the center of public life on the island. It was the site of lavish balls and state functions, including the historic 1864 conference on federal union. The provincial

legislature still convenes here; meetings are in session between mid-February and early May for 5 to 17 weeks, depending on how much provincial government haggling is underway.

In the late 1970s, Parks Canada undertook restoration of the age-begrimed building, a five-year task completed in 1983. Layers of paint came off the front columns. The double-hung windows throughout were refitted with glass panes from an old greenhouse in New Brunswick. About 10 percent of the original furnishings remained in the building before

Getting to Prince Edward Island

Confederation Bridge

Most visitors to Prince Edward Island arrive by road, traveling either across the Confederation Bridge or on the ferry. You can also fly to Charlottetown.

CONFEDERATION BRIDGE

The impressive Confederation Bridge (902/437-7300 or 888/437-6565, www.confederation-bridge.com) is Prince Edward Island's most important transportation link to the rest of Canada. From Cape Jourimain (New Brunswick), 80 kilometers east of Moncton, the bridge stretches across Northumberland Strait to Borden-Carleton, which is in Prince County, 60 kilometers west of Charlottetown. Driving across the impressive 12.9-kilometer span takes about 10 minutes (views are blocked by concrete barriers erected as a windbreak).

The round-trip bridge toll is $45 per vehicle, including passengers. Payment (credit card, debit card, or cash) is collected at Borden-Carleton upon leaving the island.

BY FERRY

Prince Edward Island is also linked to the rest of Atlantic Canada by ferry. The mainland departure point is Caribou (Nova Scotia), near Pictou, a two-hour drive from Halifax. The ferry docks at Wood Islands, a scenic 62-kilometer drive southeast from Charlottetown. The 75-minute crossing is operated by Northumberland Ferries (902/566-3838 or 800/565-0201, www.ferries.ca) May to mid-December, with up to nine crossings in each direction daily during peak summer season. The round-trip fare is $69 per vehicle, regardless of the number of passengers. As with the bridge crossing, payment is made upon leaving the island, so to save a few bucks, take the ferry to PEI and return on the Confederation Bridge.

BY AIR

Air Canada (888/247-2262, www.aircanada.com) has direct flights to Charlottetown from Halifax, Montréal, Ottawa, and Toronto. WestJet (403/250-5839 or 888/937-8538, www.westjet.com) flies in from Toronto.

Province House

restoration and were retained. Most of the rest were replaced by period antiques obtained in the other provinces and the northeastern United States. A flowered rug was woven for Confederation Chamber, where the Fathers of Confederation convened. Every nook and corner was refurbished and polished until the interior gleamed. Today, Province House is one of Atlantic Canada's most significant public buildings.

Confederation Centre of the Arts

Confederation Centre of the Arts (145 Richmond St., 902/628-1864) is the other half of the imposing complex shared by Province House. The promenades, edged with places to sit, are great places for people-watching, and kids like to skateboard on the walkways.

The center opened in 1964 to mark the centennial of the Charlottetown Conference, as the confederation meeting became known in Canadian history. It's a great hulk of a place, compatible with its historic neighbor in its design and coloring. The center houses an art gallery, the provincial library, four theaters, and a café. The emphasis at the

Confederation Centre Art Gallery (mid-May-Oct. daily 9am-5pm, Nov.-mid-May Wed.-Sat. 11am-5pm and Sun. 1pm-5pm; free) is the work of Canadian artists—expect to see some of island artist Robert Harris's paintings and Lucy Maud Montgomery's original manuscripts. A gift shop stocks wares by the cream of PEI's artisans.

All Souls' Chapel

A few blocks west of Queen Street, the remarkable **All Souls' Chapel** next to **St. Peter's Cathedral** (Rochford St., 902/566-2102; daily 8am-6pm; free) was a joint Harris family creation. The architect William Harris styled it in island sandstone with a dark walnut interior. His brother Robert painted the murals and deftly mixed family members and friends among the religious figures.

Beaconsfield Historic House

A bright-yellow, 25-room mansion, **Beaconsfield Historic House** (2 Kent St., 902/368-6603; tours summer daily 10am-5pm, spring and fall Mon.-Fri.; adult $5, senior and child $4) was built in 1877 from a William Critchlow Harris design. The building has survived more than a century of varied use as a family home, a shelter for "friendless women," a YWCA, and a nurses' residence. It was rescued in 1973 by the PEI Museum and Heritage Foundation, which turned it into foundation headquarters and a heritage museum. A good bookstore is on the first level, and genealogical archives are kept across the hall and upstairs. The wide front porch overlooking the harbor across a long lawn is a great place to have tea and scones.

★ Victoria Park

Victoria Park, adjacent to Beaconsfield House, reigns as one of Charlottetown's prettiest settings, with 16 wooded and grassy hectares overlooking the bay at Battery Point. The greenery spreads out across the peninsula tip; to get there, follow Kent Street as it turns into Park Roadway. The park's rolling terrain is built of moraines, heaps of gravelly deposits left behind by ice-age glaciers.

Joggers like the park's winding paths, and birders find abundant yellow warblers, purple finches, and downy woodpeckers nesting in the maples, firs, oaks, pines, and birches. The

white palatial mansion overlooking the water is Fanningbank (Government House), the lieutenant governor's private residence—nice to look at, but it's closed to the public.

BEYOND DOWNTOWN

Charlottetown Farmers Market

The Charlottetown Farmers Market (100 Belvedere Ave., 902/626-3373; Sat. 9am-2pm and summer Wed. 9am-2pm) is across from the university campus. The indoor market holds about 40 vendors selling everything from flowers and crafts to baked goods, produce, and fish.

Fort Amherst-Port-la-Joye National Historic Site

Just four kilometers across the harbor from downtown but a 35-minute drive via Routes 1 and 19, Fort Amherst-Port-la-Joye National Historic Site protects the island's first European settlement. It all began in 1720, when three French ships sailed into Port-la-Joye (today's Charlottetown Harbour) carrying some 300 settlers. Most of them moved to the north shore and established fishing

Fanningbank is home to the lieutenant governor.

villages, but the rest remained here at the military outpost.

Within just four years, adverse conditions had driven out most of the French. The British burned Port-la-Joye in 1745 and took control of the island. The French later returned to rebuild their capital, but were compelled to surrender Port-la-Joye to a superior British force in 1758. The British renamed the post Fort Amherst. After the British established a new capital at Charlottetown, Fort Amherst fell quickly into disrepair, and now no buildings remain. The grounds, which have picnic tables, are open June-August.

RECREATION

Those looking for easy walking gravitate to the waterfront at the southwestern end of downtown. This is the starting point for a **paved trail** that extends to Old Battery Point and Victoria Park. While this area is also popular for biking, cyclists looking for longer rides will be impressed at how easy it is to reach the rural landscape beyond city limits. From downtown, the ride out to Brackley Beach (45 kilometers) is a good full-day ride.

MacQueen's Bike Shop (430 Queen St., 902/368-2453; Mon.-Sat. 8:30am-5:30pm, Sun. 10am-2pm) provides complete bike and accessory rental and repairs and can also arrange cycle-touring packages. **Smooth Cycle** (330 University Ave., 902/569-5690; Mon.-Thurs. 9am-5:30pm, Fri. 9am-6pm, Sat. 9am-5pm) also offers rentals and repairs, as well as drop-offs for the Confederation Trail. Both companies charge from $26-30 per day for a road bike.

Entertainment and Events

Charlottetown once rolled up the sidewalks at night, but in recent years a rousing nightlife and pub scene has emerged centered on drinking and dancing. Last call for drinks is at 1:30am; the doors lock at 2am. For complete listings of all that's happening around the city, pick up the free weekly *Buzz* (www.buzzon.com) or the weekend editions of *The Guardian* (http://www.theguardian.pe.ca).

NIGHTLIFE

Peake's Quay (1 Great George St., 902/368-1330; daily from 11am) has a prime waterfront location, making it popular with both locals and visitors. While the service is often indifferent, it's a good family-friendly environment with inexpensive food and lots of outdoor seating. Look for live music most weekends after 9pm. **Olde Dublin Pub** (131 Sydney St., 902/892-6992; Mon.-Wed. 11am-midnight, Thurs.-Sat. 11am-2am) has a popular deck and offers Celtic and Irish music Thursday-Saturday for a small cover charge.

Mavor's (145 Richmond St., 902/628-6107; Mon.-Sat. 11am-midnight), in the Confederation Centre of the Arts, is a colorful space with more than 40 wines by the glass, top-notch martinis, and a thoughtful menu of light meals under $20.

Water's Edge Bar (Delta Prince Edward, 18 Queen St., 902/894-1208; Sun.-Thurs. 11am-11pm, Fri.-Sat. 11am-midnight) is a sophisticated space within one of the city's top hotels. The highlight for beer-lovers is a long list of regional brews.

The Brickhouse (125 Sydney St., 902/566-4620; Sun.-Thurs. 11am-10pm, Fri.-Sat. 11am-11pm) is another good choice for a quiet drink and conversation. Located in an 1850s building where the timber-frame and red brick is exposed, it's a stylish space that is best known as a restaurant, but there's no problem stopping by for a quiet drink at the bar or heading upstairs to the more private lounge (Thurs.-Sat. from 6pm).

A mainstay of the live music scene is

Peake's Quay

Baba's Lounge (upstairs at 81 University Ave., 902/892-7377; Mon.-Thurs. 11am-11pm, Fri.-Sat. 11am-midnight, Sun. 5pm-midnight), a popular hangout with the younger set since the earlier 1990s. "Intimate" is an understatement here; bodies writhe to the rhythm on a dance floor about the size of a postage stamp. Expect live music ranging from slightly alternative to modern rock.

PERFORMING ARTS

The **Confederation Centre of the Arts** (145 Richmond St., 902/566-1267) is the performing arts capital of the province and the site of the **Charlottetown Festival** (www.charlottetownfestival.com), which runs from mid-June to late September. The festival is best known for the *Anne of Green Gables* musical; tickets cost $50-70. Also on the bill are repertory productions in the center's main theater and cabaret-style productions at the **MacKenzie Theatre,** the festival's second stage (University Ave. and Grafton St.).

June

The mid-June to mid-October **Charlottetown Festival** (902/566-1267, www.charlottetownfestival.com) presents musical theater and cabaret at the Confederation Centre and the nearby MacKenzie Theatre. Two musicals are presented, including one centering on *Anne of Green Gables*.

July

The **Canada Day** long weekend (first weekend in July) is celebrated on the waterfront with a food fair, nationalistic displays, buskers, island music, and the **Festival of Lights** fireworks display.

Organized by the Charlottetown Yacht Club, **Race Week** (902/892-9065, www.cyc.pe.ca) runs Wednesday-Saturday in the middle of July. The program revolves around yacht races for various classes of boats, with other scheduled activities including shore games and nightly entertainment. Even if you're not involved in the event, watching the yachts racing across the harbor is a sight to behold.

August

The mid-August **Old Home Week** (902/629-6623, www.oldhomeweekpei.com), Atlantic Canada's largest agricultural exposition, centers on Charlottetown Driving Park, northeast of downtown along Kensington Road. The city unofficially shuts down for the week-ending **Gold Cup Parade** through the streets of Charlottetown—said to be Atlantic Canada's biggest and best-attended parade. Daily grounds admission is a reasonable adult $12, child $5.

September
★ **INTERNATIONAL SHELLFISH FESTIVAL**

Summer ends with the **International Shellfish Festival** (www.peishellfish.com), over the third weekend of September.

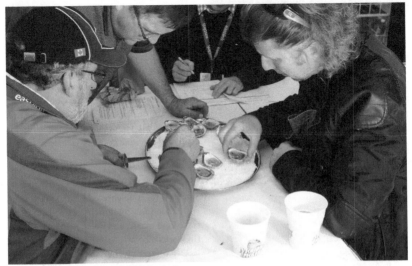

judging at the International Shellfish Festival

Festivities along the waterfront include an oyster-shucking contest, a Chowder Challenge, "touch tanks," cooking classes, the World Is Your Oyster children's program, sock-hanging, and chefs from the local culinary institute sharing their cooking skills with the public.

Shopping

Centrally located and PEI's largest city by far, Charlottetown is the island's shopping hub. Downtown is a pleasant blend of old and new shopping experiences, although the main concentration of shopping malls is north of downtown along University Avenue. Stores catering to islanders are normally open Monday-Saturday from about 9am-5pm, while touristy ones open later in July and August and also operate on Sunday.

ARTS AND CRAFTS

Local artists capture the island in masterful watercolors, acrylics, oils, and sculpture. Local crafts include finely made quilts, knits and woolens, stained glass, jewelry, pewter, pottery, and handsome furniture. The Anne doll is the most popular souvenir, and it's produced in innumerable variations for as little as $20 to as much as $800.

An exquisite handmade quilt costs $400-800—seldom a bargain. But well-crafted quilts are sturdily constructed and will last a lifetime with good care. Sweaters ($75-300) are especially high quality. One of the best sources is **Northern Watters Knitwear,** which operates a downtown factory outlet (150 Richmond St., 902/566-5850; Mon.-Fri. 9am-6pm, closed Sat., Sun. 11:30am-5pm).

The **PEI Crafts Council** (www.peicrafts-council.com) is a driving force behind local arts and crafts. It counts about 100 provincial craftspeople among its esteemed ranks. A visit to their website shows all members and the variety of their products (quilts, glassware, sculpture, clothing, knitted apparel, and jewelry ad infinitum), and provides a list of markets and craft shows they attend.

Accommodations and Camping

You'll find every kind of lodging, from plain budget places to sumptuous expensive rooms, in Charlottetown's 100-plus lodgings. Also, unlike elsewhere in the province, most are open year-round.

Unless noted otherwise, prices given are for a double room; sales tax is not included.

DOWNTOWN
Under $50
The city's lone hostel is the HI-affiliated **Charlottetown Backpackers** (60 Hillsborough St., 902/367-5749, www.charlottetownbackpackers.com; dorm beds $28-32, $71-79 d), a converted residential home two blocks east of Province House. Facilities include a living room with a fireplace, bike rentals, a recreation room, and wireless Internet.

$50-100
In the vicinity of the hostel is another cheapie—**Aloha Tourist Home** (234 Sydney St., 902/892-5642 or 855/892-5642, www.alohaamigo.com; $89-225 s or d), an inexpensive downtown accommodation for those looking for private rooms. The renovated home has six guest rooms with single or double beds, two shared bathrooms, a shared kitchen, a lounge area, and free wireless Internet throughout. The least expensive rooms share bathrooms, while the others have en suites.

One of the least expensive of Charlottetown's historic accommodations with en suite rooms is **MacInnis Bed and Breakfast** (80 Euston St., 902/892-6725), a homey, centrally located choice with a veranda that overlooks pleasant gardens. It offers two regular guest rooms ($85 s or d) and a top-floor one-bedroom suite ($135 s or d), all decorated in a distinctive Victorian style.

$100-150
The elegant 1860s ★ **Shipwright Inn** (51 Fitzroy St., 902/368-1905 or 888/306-9966, www.shipwrightinn.com; $149-299 s or d) was originally the home of shipbuilder James Douse. The inn has eight rooms and suites, all with private baths and furnished in richly colored nautical themes (my favorite is the Chart Room, with an 1830s four-poster walnut bed, heavy drapes, and historic sea charts on the walls). Rates include a full breakfast.

What makes **Elmwood Heritage Inn** (121 North River Rd., 902/368-3310 or 877/933-3310, www.elmwoodinn.pe.ca; $159-279 s or d including breakfast) stand out is the setting. Still within easy walking distance of downtown, its parklike grounds are surrounded by mature gardens; a row of stately elm trees leads up from the wrought-iron entry gates to the front door. Built for the grandson of Samuel Cunard in 1889, the mansion boasts 28 very Victorian guest rooms, many with jetted tubs and fireplaces.

Best Western Charlottetown (238 Grafton St., 902/892-2461 or 800/528-1234, www.bestwesternatlantic.com; $145-185 s or d includes a hot breakfast) is a three-block jaunt from Province House. It has 143 mid-sized rooms fronting both sides of the street. Facilities include an indoor pool, fitness center, hot tub, and launderette.

$150-200
A restored Queen Anne Revival mansion awash with antiques, **Dundee Arms** (200 Pownal St., 902/892-2496 or 877/638-6333, www.eden.travel; $155-220 s, $165-230 d) has been taking in guests since the early 1970s. Conveniently located between downtown and Victoria Park, its other pluses include a good restaurant and comfortable beds. Note that half the 22 rooms are in a modern addition behind the original home, but these are still stylishly decorated and come with wireless Internet, bathrobes, and more.

Charlotte's Rose Inn (11 Grafton St.,

www.charlottesrose.com, 902/892-3699 or 888/237-3699; April-Oct.; $175-195 s or d) is a three-story 1884 home on a quiet residential street. Original hardwood floors, high ceilings, and Victorian-era furnishings add to the charm. Rates include a hot breakfast, wireless Internet, and use of bikes.

Over $200

A few steps from Province House, ★ The Great George (58 Great George St., 902/892-0606 or 800/361-1118, www.thegreatgeorge.com; $225-375 s or d) comprises 60 guest rooms spread through 15 beautifully restored buildings from as early as 1811. The lobby is in a building that was originally known as the Pavilion Hotel, at the corner of Great George and Sydney Streets. It was here that the Fathers of Confederation stayed during the 1864 Charlottetown Conference. This building also has a large lounge area and a fine-dining restaurant. Rooms in this and buildings running up Great George Street and beyond have been beautifully restored, with the addition of modern amenities like air-conditioning and wireless Internet.

Extensive renovations have transformed the old Islander motel into the ★ Hotel on Pownal (146 Pownal St., 902/892-1217 or 800/268-6261, www.thehotelonpownal.com; $240 s or d), offering chic boutique lodging. The 45 guest rooms are smartly decorated and filled with modern amenities, including extra-large wall-mounted TVs, iPod docking stations, and wireless Internet. Comfortable beds, luxurious bathrooms, and free continental breakfast round out this popular downtown lodging.

Rodd Charlottetown (75 Kent St., 902/894-7371 or 800/565-7633, www.rodd-vacations.com; from $245 s or d) is a grand red-brick 1931 Georgian gem with magnificent woodwork and furnishings made by island craftspeople. It offers 115 rooms and suites and a restaurant, whirlpool, indoor pool, and rooftop patio. As always with these top-end properties, check the website for the best deals.

Rodd Charlottetown

Like the nearby Confederation Centre, the Delta Prince Edward (18 Queen St., 902/566-2222 or 888/890-3222, www.delta-hotels.com; $250 s or d) stands out for its boxy look amid the gracious buildings of downtown. Inside are 211 well-decorated rooms. The more expensive Delta Rooms have king beds and water views. It offers all the amenities of a full-service hotel, including underground valet parking, a day spa, a fitness room, an indoor pool, a lounge, and a restaurant. Disregard the rack rates and check online—you should find packages that include accommodations and either theater tickets or greens fees for around $200 d.

NORTH OF DOWNTOWN

Staying downtown has its perks, but if you're looking for a well-priced motel room or are traveling with a family, staying on the north side is a good alternative.

$50-100

Out near the airport, Fair Isle Motel (Rte. 2,

902/368-8259 or 800/309-8259, www.fairisle-pei.com; Apr.-Nov.; $80-125 s or d) is an old roadside motel where rooms overlook landscaped gardens and a small playground. All rooms have wireless Internet and basic cooking facilities. If you've picked up fresh seafood at Lobster on the Wharf, take advantage of this motel's barbecues for a great outdoor dinner.

I doubt too many Canadian capitals boast a cottage complex surrounded by expansive lawns within city limits, but Charlottetown does, in the form of ★ **Royalty Maples Cottages & Motel** (Rte. 2, 902/368-1030 or 800/831-7829, www.royaltymaples.com; May-Nov.), which is one kilometer north of the junction of Routes 1 and 2. The 10 one- and two-bedroom cottages ($99-169 s or d) each have a full kitchen, living area, and air-conditioning. Six motel rooms also go for $80-120 s or d per night.

$150-200

At the busy intersection of Routes 1 and 2, north of downtown along University Avenue, is **Rodd Royalty** (14 Capital Dr., 902/894-8566 or 800/565-7633, www.roddvacations.

com; $145-190 s or d). This spread-out property features 119 standard rooms and suites (the latter are better value). Other facilities include an indoor pool with a long waterslide, a fitness room, and a restaurant.

The **Holiday Inn Express** (200 TransCanada Hwy., 902/892-1201 or 800/465-4329, www.ihg.com; $165-210 s or d) maintains the same standards and facilities expected of this worldwide chain. The modern rooms have air-conditioning and high-speed Internet access, and rates include a continental breakfast. Families can take advantage of children's suites, complete with Nintendo systems and bunk beds separate from the main bedroom. Other amenities include an indoor pool and a sundeck.

CAMPGROUNDS
West

★ **Cornwall/Charlottetown KOA** (208 Ferry Rd., off Rte. 248, 2 km east of Cornwall, 902/566-2421, www.koa.com; June-early Oct.; $32) spreads across 25 beautiful hectares along the West River. Amenities include an outdoor swimming pool, a playground, hayrides, showers, a launderette, and a kitchen shelter.

Food

Island fare is *good,* and while it centers on homegrown produce and seafood from the surrounding ocean, everything comes together in the capital, where you'll find an excellent array of dining opportunities for all budgets. The center of the eating action is **Victoria Row,** a block of vintage buildings along Richmond Street between Queen and Great George Streets. The street is pedestrian-only through summer. The restaurants set up outdoor tables while musicians play to the assembled crowd of diners.

Even if you're not in town for the **International Shellfish Festival** (third weekend of Sept.), you'll find local delicacies such as lobster and Malpeque oysters on

menus throughout the city. Local produce and dairy products are delicious. Chefs make the most of island-grown succulent berries, locally produced maple syrup, and thick, sweet honey.

CAFÉS

What began with a German couple selling homemade bread to a local farmers market has morphed into **Leonhard's** (42 University Ave., 902/367-3621; Mon.-Sun. 9am-5pm; lunches $5.50-13), a cozy café where the emphasis is on hearty yet healthy European-style cooking. Look for mouthwatering French toast and Bavarian-style omelets for breakfast; at lunch, the delicious gluten-free soups are made from scratch, or choose the smoked turkey focaccia.

A couple of doors down from Leonhard's, **Beanz Espresso Bar** (38 University Ave., 902/892-8797; Mon.-Sat. 6:30am-6pm; $7-12) gets rave reviews for its coffee, but the soups, salads, sandwiches, and old-fashioned pastries draw me back every time I'm in Charlottetown.

One block north of the two places recommended above, **Cafe Thomas Martin** (98 Fitzroy St., 902/892-0809; Mon.-Fri. 8am-3pm; lunches $6-10) is a friendly place far enough away from the main tourist attractions that it is missed by most tourists. On the menu are dozens of hot drink choices, light lunches such as chowders and sandwiches, and a tempting array of sweet treats.

At the Confederation Centre of the Arts, ★ **Mavor's** (145 Richmond St., 902/628-6107; daily 8am-8pm; lunches $8-15) is a striking room where you can get your fill of Starbucks coffee. The kitchen opens daily (except Sunday) at 11am, serving up fresh and wholesome food, with ethnic influences showing through in dishes such as blue mussels steamed in Thai curry broth. Also good: the thin-crust smoked salmon pizza and sweet potato wedges with a side of sour cream.

If you like old-fashioned diners with menus to match the era, sidle up to a booth or the counter at **Linda's Coffee Shop** (32 Queen St., 902/892-7292; Mon.-Fri. 7am-2:30pm, Sat.-Sun. 8am-2:30pm; lunches $6-11).

SEAFOOD

★ **Water Prince Corner Shop** (141 Water St., 902/368-3212; May-Oct. daily 9am-8pm, July-Aug. until 10pm; $15-28) looks like a regular convenience store from the outside, but inside the ocean-blue clapboard building is a casual dining space where the emphasis is on fresh seafood at reasonable prices. It's all good—lobster burgers, lobster dinners with potato salad and mussels, Malpeque oysters, seafood chowder, steamed clams, and more.

For its harbor-front location alone, **Lobster on the Wharf** (2 Prince St.,

Beanz Espresso Bar

902/368-2888; May-Oct. 11:30am-10pm; $17-33) is a longtime favorite with visitors and locals alike. It has well over 300 seats, with more than 100 of these outside on multi-tiered decks built over the water. As the name suggests, lobster is the specialty (the two-person Lobster Feed is a local favorite), but the fish-and-chips and baked halibut are also excellent.

Fishbones (136 Richmond St., 902/628-6569; May-Oct. daily 11am-midnight; $17-25) is a fresh, casual restaurant along pedestrian-only Victoria Row. Start at the oyster bar before moving on to a set menu of contemporary creations, such as butter salmon curry. Other highlights include lobster mac and cheese, grilled halibut with mango salsa, and fish tacos.

The ★ **Claddagh Oyster House** (131 Sydney St., 902/892-9661; Mon.-Sat. 5pm-10pm, Sun. 5pm-9pm; $27-34) is authentically Irish, starting with owner Liam Dolan from County Galway. Local oysters dominate the menu and come in many forms (including a tasting platter of 25 for $70). Seafood is the specialty on the main menu, with the fresh lobster a rich-tasting splurge.

PUBS

Taking full advantage of its harbor-front locale is the upstairs **Peake's Quay** (1 Great George St., 902/368-1330; daily from 11am; $13-24), with informal indoor and outdoor dining and an enviable seafood selection; try the scallops sauced with honey butter. Peake's Quay is also arguably the hottest nightspot in town, drawing locals, landlubber tourists, and yachties (who tie up at the adjacent marina) alike to see and be seen while listening or dancing to top touring bands, so plan on dining early.

The Merchantman Pub (23 Queen St., 902/892-9150; Mon.-Sat. from 11:30am; $16-28) has a nice atmosphere, a wide-ranging menu that includes some Thai and Cajun dishes, and a good beer selection. But the place seems a little overpriced, probably because of its location across the street from the upscale Delta Prince Edward.

CANADIAN

The **Lucy Maud Dining Room** (4 Sydney St., 902/894-6868; summer Tues.-Sat. 5:30-8:30pm, the rest of the year Tues.-Fri. 11:30am-1pm and Tues.-Sat. 5:30-8:30pm; $22-35) is the training restaurant for the Culinary Institute of Canada, a respected school that attracts students from across the country. Turn a blind eye to the rather institutional room, concentrate on the water views, and sit back to enjoy enthusiastic service and well-priced meals that blend contemporary and Continental cuisine.

Take a break from seafood by making reservations at ★ **Sims Corner** (86 Queen St., 902/894-7467; daily 11:30am-10:30pm; $18-35), the island's only true steakhouse. Ensconced in a historic 1860s red-brick building, the subtle setting is the perfect place to indulge in island-raised beef cooked exactly as ordered. For the full effect, choose a robust red from the extensive wine list and end your

meal with a slab of dark chocolate brownie parfait.

If you want to dine in one of the city's best restaurants, but don't want to pay for an expensive dinner, eat breakfast at **The Selkirk** (Delta Prince Edward, 18 Queen St., 902/894-1208; daily 7am-9pm; $19-33). The buffet is $17, or try dishes as traditional as blueberry muffins or as creative as crab and lobster scrambled tortilla pie. Things go upscale in the evening: That's when you can order pork tenderloin ravioli or smoked duck and asparagus salad to start, followed by sturgeon grilled in a cilantro-lime butter or a chilled seafood platter for two.

The **Griffon Room** (Dundee Arms, 200 Pownal St., 902/892-2496; daily for breakfast, lunch, and dinner; $22-33) is away from the tourist crush within a restored three-story manor that combines an old-fashioned setting with elegantly conceived fine cuisine emphasizing red meats and seafood. If you feel like a break from seafood, you won't regret the mint-rubbed rack of lamb.

ITALIAN

Sirenella Ristorante (83 Water St., 902/628-2271; Mon.-Fri. 11:30am-2pm, Mon.-Sat. 5pm-10pm; $17-28) serves up traditional northern Italian food in the simple surrounds of a small yellow building set back from busy Water Street. The veal dishes are tempting, but order the scallop and wild mushroom pappardelle for your fill of local produce. The wine list is dominated by Italian reds and whites.

ICE CREAM

Dairy fanciers whoop it up at ★ **Cow's,** a local ice cream company that is renowned as much for its creamy treats wrapped in handmade waffle cones as for its colorful merchandise. Downtown outlets include one opposite the Confederation Centre (corner of Queen St. and Grafton St., 902/892-6969) and at Peake's Wharf (902/566-4886). On your way off the island, you can also indulge at Gateway Village or aboard the ferry.

Information and Services

The provincial **Visitor Information Centre** is inside the lobby of Founders' Hall (6 Prince St., 902/368-4444; May daily 9am-5pm, June daily 9am-6pm, July-Aug. daily 8:30am-6pm, Sept. daily 8:30am-5pm, Oct. daily 9am-4pm). The staff answers questions and stocks a good supply of literature about the province and Charlottetown.

Queen Elizabeth Hospital is on Riverside Drive (902/894-2200). For **police** call 902/566-7112.

Transportation

GETTING THERE

Air

Charlottetown Airport (250 Maple Hills Ave., 902/566-7997, www.flypei.com) is eight kilometers north of downtown along Brackley Point Road. The airport has a restaurant, gift shop, seasonal visitor center, and wireless Internet (for a fee). Taxis wait outside during flight arrivals and charge $11 for one person or $14 for two for the 15-minute drive to town. Avis, Budget, Hertz, and National rent vehicles at the airport, but their counters are not staffed between flights. **Air Canada** (888/247-2262) has direct flights from Toronto, Montréal, Ottawa, and Halifax, while **WestJet** (888/937-8538) flies in from Toronto.

Car

From Moncton, it's a little more than 160 kilometers (two hours) to Charlottetown via Route 15 and the Confederation Bridge.

Ferry

From Caribou, a short drive north of Pictou, **Northumberland Ferries** (902/566-3838 or 800/565-0201, www.ferries.ca) operates 5-9 sailings May-mid-December daily to the eastern side of Prince Edward Island. The trip takes just over an hour, and the fare is $69 round-trip per vehicle, regardless of the number of passengers (you pay when leaving the island).

GETTING AROUND

Use **Charlottetown Transit** (902/566-9962) to get anywhere in Greater Charlottetown for adult $2.25, child $1; buses run weekdays only.

Charlottetown taxis are plentiful; you'll pay $6-10 to get almost anywhere downtown. Taxis cruise the streets or wait at major downtown hotels. Taxi companies include **City Cab** (902/892-6567), **Co-op** (902/892-1111), and **Yellow Cab** (902/566-6666).

Local rental car agencies include **Avis** (902/892-3706), **Budget** (902/566-5525), **Hertz** (902/966-5566), and **National** (902/628-6990).

Boat Tours

Peake's Wharf Boat Tours (1 Great George St., 902/629-1864, www.peakeswharfboat-tours.com) operates a covered 42-foot boat from Peake's Wharf, at the foot of Great George Street. Options include a 2.5-hour seal-watching cruise (2:30pm; adult $44) and 70-minute evening and sunset cruises (6:30pm and 8pm; both adult $30). The tours run June-early September, with children half the adult price.

The South Shore

From Charlottetown, Route 1 (TransCanada Highway) whisks travelers 56 kilometers southwest to Borden-Carleton, where the Confederation Bridge provides a link to the rest of Canada. If you're arriving on the island via the bridge, consider veering off Route 1 at DeSable and following scenic Route 19 along the South Shore to Rocky Point and Fort Amherst-Port-la-Joye National Historic Site for views of the city skyline across sparkling Charlottetown Harbour.

VICTORIA

Victoria (pop. 200), 40 kilometers west of Charlottetown, marks Queens County's southwestern corner. The town owed its start to shipbuilding, and by 1870 Victoria ranked as one of the island's busiest ports. As the demand for wooden ships faded, the seaport turned to cattle shipping—herds of cattle were driven down the coastal slopes to water's edge, where they were hoisted with slings onto waiting ships.

Today Victoria shows just a spark of its former luster. The seaport slipped off the commercial circuit decades ago, and the settlement shrank to a handful of waterfront blocks. Happily, island craftspeople discovered the serene setting. It's still a quiet place where the fishing fleet puts out to sea early in the morning as the mist rises off the strait. But now the peaceful seaport also holds a modest arts colony, with outlets along the main street.

Victoria Playhouse

If an evening at the theater sounds good, make plans to attend the Victoria Playhouse (Howard St., 902/658-2025, www.victoria-playhouse.com; adult $32, senior $30, child $21.50), a repertory theater that showcases historically themed comedy and drama, as well as concerts of jazz and folk music.

Accommodations and Food

Next to the Victoria Playhouse, Victoria Village Inn (Howard St., 902/658-2483 or 866/658-2483, www.victoriavillageinn.com; $100-155 s or d) is an 1870s inn that was originally built for a sea captain. Awash with lustrous antiques, it offers four comfortable guest units—one with three bedrooms.

Kitty-corner to the theater, the Orient Hotel (34 Main St., 902/658-2503 or 800/565-6743, www.theorienthotel.com; mid-May-mid-Oct.; $95-160 s or d) has been taking in guests since 1900. It features a few smallish guest rooms and three larger suites (from $125). Rates include a delicious breakfast and tea and coffee throughout the day.

Enterprising locals remodeled the old general store and post office and opened ★ Landmark Café (12 Main St., 902/658-2286; June-Sept. daily 11:30am-2:45pm and 5pm-9:30pm; $11-22). You can't go wrong with any of the fresh seasonal cooking, but the soups and meat pies are especially good.

Getting There

To get to Victoria from Charlottetown, it's a 35-kilometer (25-minute) drive along Route 1.

BORDEN-CARLETON

The twin villages of Borden-Carleton, 56 kilometers west of Charlottetown, are the closest point of the island to mainland Canada, and so have always been an important transportation hub. Back in the late 1700s, iceboats carrying mail and passengers crossed Northumberland Strait when the island was icebound from December to early spring. The voyages generated hair-raising tales of survival, and the iceboats—rigged with fragile sails and runners—were often trapped in the strait's ice. It wasn't until 1916 that the first vehicle ferry made the crossing. In 1997, the

Confederation Bridge opened and the ferry service was discontinued. Since the opening of the bridge, Borden-Carleton has seen much development, as thousands of travelers peeling off the bridge come looking for food and information, and those leaving stop to stock up on last-minute souvenirs.

Gateway Village

As you descend the final span of Confederation Bridge, 12-hectare Gateway Village soon comes into view down on the right. It is designed especially for bridge travelers, but it's worth visiting even if you're on your way back to the mainland. Designed on the theme of an island streetscape of the early 1900s, the shops are filled with island souvenirs, some tacky (T-shirts, Christmas decorations), some tasty (fresh lobster), and some trendy (wine from Rossignol Estate Winery). The epicenter for new arrivals is the cavernous Gateway Village Visitor Information Centre (902/437-8570; winter daily 9am-6pm, spring and fall daily 9am-8pm, summer daily 9am-10pm), where friendly staff will help sort out the best way to spend your time on the island. Displays focus on various island experiences. Outside, amid the café tables and wandering visitors, free musical performances and craft demonstrations add to the appeal.

Marine Rail Park

From the heart of Gateway Village, head south toward Northumberland Strait on Carleton Street and turn right on Borden Avenue to reach Marine Rail Park. Until the bridge was completed in 1997, this was where ferries from the mainland docked, and today the area has been converted to a green space. Interpretive boards tell the story of the former ferry service, but the best reason to visit the park is for unobstructed views of the Confederation Bridge.

Accommodations

A few kilometers east of Borden-Carleton toward Charlottetown, Carleton Motel (TransCanada Hwy., 902/437-3030, www.carletonmotelpei.com; $65-90 s or d) offers 22 basic rooms, some with cooking facilities; a small adjacent café is open daily from 7am to around 3pm.

★ Lord's Seaside Cottages (Bells Point Rd., off Rte. 10, 902/437-2426 or 888/228-6765, www.lordsseasidecottages.com; June-Sept.; $160 s or d per night in spring and fall, $1,000 per week in July and Aug.) is well worth the extra money. Sitting on Bells Point, a few kilometers west of Borden-Carleton, the eight simple cottages each have 1-3 bedrooms, a TV, and a deck with a barbecue—an excellent deal for families or couples traveling together.

Getting There

From Charlottetown, it's 55 kilometers (40 minutes) to Borden-Carleton via Route 1.

CROSSING THE CONFEDERATION BRIDGE

If you arrived in Borden-Carleton via the Confederation Bridge, you enjoyed a free ride. If you're leaving the island, it's time to pay. The toll is $45 per vehicle, including passengers. Payment is collected at toll booths on the island side of the bridge. Have cash, a credit card, or a debit card ready.

Charlottetown to Cavendish

The most direct route between Charlottetown and Cavendish is to take Route 2 west from the capital for 25 kilometers, and then head north from Hunter River on Route 13. It takes less than one hour to reach the coast. This more leisurely alternative (1.5 hours) begins by taking Route 2 northeast from Charlottetown to Grand Tracadie and then following Route 6 west along the coast to Cavendish. If you've been traveling through Kings County (on Eastern Prince Edward Island), Tracadie Cross, the turnoff for the coastal route, is just seven kilometers west of Mount Stewart.

GRAND TRACADIE

Grand Tracadie is about 40 minutes from Charlottetown. It is the eastern gateway to Prince Edward Island National Park, but it is best known for a historic inn that lies within the park, two kilometers from the town center.

Accommodations and Food

Elegant green-roofed ★ Dalvay by the Sea (16 Cottage Lane, 902/672-2048 or 888/366-2955, www.dalvaybythesea.com; mid-June–early Oct.; $200-280 s or d, including breakfast) appeals to guests who like an old-money ambience. The rustic mansion was built in 1895 by millionaire American oil industrialist Alexander MacDonald, who used the lodging as a summer retreat. Today the hotel, its antiques, and its spacious grounds are painstakingly maintained by the national park staff. Eight three-bedroom cottages on the grounds ($400-420 d, including breakfast) are most popular with families.

The hotel's dining room is locally renowned, and nonguests are welcome with advance reservations. Entrées ($22-38) feature formal Canadian cuisine prepared with a French flair. The emphasis is on the freshest produce, best seafood, and finest beef cuts. Mains include rack of lamb crusted with hazelnut and grainy mustard; the sticky date pudding topped with toffee sauce is an easy choice for dessert. Other hotel facilities

Dalvay by the Sea is one of the island's premier lodgings.

include a well-stocked gift shop, a nearby beach, a tennis court, bike rentals, a lake with canoes, and nature trails.

Getting There

Grand Tracadie is a little over 20 kilometers (15 minutes) northeast of Charlottetown via Route 2 and Route 6.

BRACKLEY BEACH

With its proximity to the national park, excellent beaches, golf, deep-sea fishing, and other attractions, Brackley Beach is a popular base.

Just south of town is Dunes Studio Gallery and Cafe (Brackley Point Rd., 902/672-2586; June-Oct. daily 10am-6pm), an architecturally distinctive building with the ocean-facing wall composed almost entirely of windows. Inside, a wide spiral walkway passes the work of some 70 artists, including island craftspeople who create stoneware, framed photography, gold jewelry, pottery, watercolors, woodcarvings, oils, and sculptures. It's worth browsing just for porcelains crafted by owner Peter Jansons. Make sure you find your way up to the rooftop garden.

Accommodations and Camping

Distinctive red-and-white ★ Shaw's Hotel (99 Apple Tree Rd., 902/672-2022, www.shawshotel.ca; June-mid-Oct.; $145-230 s or d) overlooks the bay from a 30-hectare peninsula at the edge of Prince Edward Island National Park. This was the Shaw family's homestead in the 1860s, and it's still in the family, now protected as a national historic site. The property has 16 antique-furnished guest rooms in the main house, 25 adjacent historic cottages, and 15 newer upscale waterfront chalets. In high season, rates start at $145 s or d for a room only; in the off-season, you can pay from $120 per person to include breakfast and dinner. The ambience is informal and friendly—a nice place for meeting islanders and other visitors. The hotel dining room (June-mid-Oct.; daily 8am-10am and 6pm-9pm; $24-36) is consistently good; start with a chowder appetizer

and stick to the chef's daily choices, prepared from whatever seafood is in season.

Camping is available nearby at the 12-hectare Vacationland Travel Park (east of Rte. 15, overlooking Brackley Bay, 902/672-2317 or 800/529-0066, www.vacationlandrv.pe.ca; mid-May-mid-Sept.; $35-39). Facilities include a convenience store, launderette, heated pool, hot showers, mini-golf, and other recreational activities.

Food

For its stylish setting, sweeping views, and creative dishes, the restaurant within the ★ Dunes Cafe (Brackley Point Rd., 902/672-2586; June-Sept. daily 11:30am-9pm, Oct. daily 11:30am-2:30pm; $27-38) is one of the best places to eat on Prince Edward Island. Seating choices are in a sunken area at the rear of the gallery or on a higher level overlooking the garden. Regardless of your preference, you will most definitely need reservations for either lunch or dinner any time through July and August. Lunches are priced from $9 to $16 and include a cold-water seafood stew and a grilled lamb burger. In the evening, both the seafood chowder and brie and pear pizza can't be faulted as starters, while for a main, the banana bread-crumbed halibut is hard to pass up.

Getting There

Brackley Beach is about 15 kilometers (10 minutes) west of Grand Tracadie via Route 6. To get there directly from Charlottetown, take Route 15 north from the Charlottetown Airport for about 15 kilometers (10 minutes).

★ PRINCE EDWARD ISLAND NATIONAL PARK

The sandy beaches, dunes, sandstone cliffs, marshes, and forestlands of Prince Edward Island National Park represent the island as it once was, unspoiled by 20th-century development.

The park protects a slender 40-kilometer-long coastal slice of natural perfection, extending almost the full length of Queens County, as well as a six-square-kilometer spit of land farther east, near Greenwich on the North Shore of eastern Prince Edward Island. The park also extends inland at Cavendish to include Green Gables Heritage Place and Green Gables Golf Course. The main body of the park is book-ended by two large bays. At the eastern end, Tracadie Bay spreads out like an oversize pond with shimmering waters. Forty kilometers to the west, New London Bay forms almost a mirror image of the eastern end. In between, long barrier islands define Rustico and Covehead Bays, and sand dunes webbed with marram grass, rushes, fragrant bayberry, and wild roses front the coastline.

Sunrise and sunset here are cast in glowing colors. All along the gulf at sunrise, the beaches have a sense of primeval peacefulness, their sands textured like herringbone by the overnight sea breezes.

Getting around is easy. Route 6 lies on the park's inland side, connecting numerous park entrances, and the Gulf Shore Parkway runs along the coast nearly the park's entire length. You can drive through the park year-round. Cyclists will appreciate the smooth wide shoulders and light traffic along the Gulf Shore Parkway.

Park Entry

Between early June and mid-September, a one-day pass is adult $8, senior $7, child $4, to a maximum of $16 per vehicle. Before purchasing a pass, check with your Cavendish accommodation, as some local lodgings include a park pass in their rates.

Environmental Factors

The national park was established in 1937 to protect the fragile dunes along the Gulf of St. Lawrence and cultural features such as Green Gables Heritage Place. Parks Canada walks a fine line, balancing environmental concerns with the responsibilities of hosting half a million park visitors a year. Boardwalks route visitors through dunes to the beaches and preserve the fragile landscape.

Bird-watchers will be amply rewarded with sightings of some of the more than 100 species known to frequent the park. Brackley Marsh, Orby Head, and the Rustico Island Causeway are good places to start. The park preserves nesting habitat for some 25 pairs of endangered piping plovers—small, shy shorebirds that arrive in early April to breed in flat sandy areas near the high-tide line. Some beaches may be closed in spring and summer when the plovers are nesting; it's vital to the birds' survival that visitors stay clear of these areas.

Recreation

The park's unbroken stretches of sandy beaches—some white, others tinted pink by iron oxide—are among the best in Atlantic Canada. On warm summer days, droves of sunbathers laze on the shore and swim in the usually gentle surf. The busier beaches have a lifeguard on duty, but always be aware of undertows.

Stanhope Beach, opposite the campground, is wide and flat and remains relatively busy throughout summer. Next up to the east, **Brackley Beach** is backed by higher sand dunes. The adjacent visitor center has changing rooms and a snack bar. **Cavendish Beach** is the busiest of all; those toward Orby Head are backed by steep red-sandstone cliffs.

Established **hiking trails** range from the 0.5-kilometer wheelchair-accessible Reeds and Rushes Trail, beginning at the Dalvay Administration Building near Grand Tracadie, to the 8-kilometer Homestead Trail beginning near the entrance to Cavendish Campground. The latter wends inland alongside freshwater ponds and through woods and marshes and is open to both hikers and bikers. Be wary of potentially hazardous cliff edges and of the poison ivy and ticks that lurk in the ground cover.

If you'd like to learn more about the park's ecology, join one of the **nature walks** led by Parks Canada rangers. The treks lead through white spruce stunted by winter storms and winds, to freshwater ponds, and into the habitats of such native animal species as red fox, northern phalarope, Swainson's thrush, and junco.

Camping

The park's two campgrounds are distinctly different from one another. A percentage of sites can be reserved through the **Parks Canada Campground Reservation Service** (877/737-3783, www.pccamping.ca) for $11 per reservation. During July and August, especially for weekends, reservations are recommended. The remaining sites are offered on a first-come, first-served basis.

Stanhope Campground (north of Stanhope; early June-early Oct.) is across the road from the ocean and has 95 unserviced sites ($28), 16 sites with two-way hookups ($33), and 14 sites with full hookups ($36). Amenities include showers, a playground, a grocery store, laundry facilities, and wooded tent sites.

Closest to Cavendish and the center of the park's summer interpretive program is **Cavendish Campground** (early June-early Oct.). This, the most popular of the three campgrounds, has 230 unserviced sites ($28)

and 78 hookup sites ($36). Campground facilities include a grocery store, kitchen shelters, launderettes, flush toilets, and hot showers.

Information

The main **Cavendish Visitor Information Centre** (902/672-6350; mid-May-mid-Oct. daily 9am-5pm, July-Aug. daily 8am-9pm) is combined with the province's Visitor Information Centre, 50 meters north of the Route 6 and Route 13 intersection in Cavendish. As well as offering general park information, displays depict the park's natural history and a small shop sells park-related literature and souvenirs. Another source of information is Parks Canada (www.pc.gc.ca).

Getting There

The Gulf Shore Parkway runs along the coast nearly the park's entire length, with four access points along a 12-kilometer stretch of Route 6 between Cavendish and North Rustico. You can drive through the park year-round.

The closest entrance to Charlottetown is at North Rustico, 30 kilometers (30 minutes)

Cavendish Beach

north of the capital along Routes 2, 7, and 6. Continuing north for four kilometers from North Rustico you can access the park along Cape Road. This access point is 34 kilometers (32 minutes) north of Charlottetown via Routes 2, 7, and then 6. The main park entrance is at Cavendish, 40 kilometers (40 minutes) north of Charlottetown via Routes 2 and 13. Less than one kilometer west of this entrance is Grahams Lane, which leads to the park's most popular beach. This access point is 41 kilometers (40 minutes) north of Charlottetown via Routes 2 and 13 to Cavendish and then west on Route 6.

RUSTICO BAY

A decade after the French began Port-la-Joye near Charlottetown, French settlers cut through the inland forest and settled Rustico Bay's coastline. England's Acadian deportation in 1755 emptied the villages, but not for long. The Acadians returned, and the five revived Rusticos—Rusticoville, Rustico, Anglo Rustico, North Rustico, and North Rustico Harbour—still thrive and encircle Rustico Bay's western shore.

Sights and Recreation

For a glimpse at Acadian culture, check out the imposing two-story **Farmers' Bank of Rustico Museum** (Church Rd., Hunter River, 902/963-3168; June-Sept. Mon.-Sat. 9:30am-5:30pm, Sun. 1pm-5pm; adult $6, senior $4.50, child $3.50). Built in 1864 as Canada's first chartered people's bank (the precursor of today's credit unions), the building served as the early Acadian banking connection, then as a library. Exhibits at this national historic site include heritage displays plus artifacts from the life of the Reverend Georges-Antoine Belcourt, the founder.

Half a dozen charter fishing operators tie up at Rustico Harbour (along the wharf behind Fisherman's Wharf Lobster Suppers). The average cost is a remarkably low $40 per person for a three-hour outing or $180 for a full day's charter; the catch includes cod, mackerel, flounder, and tuna. Most charters operate July to mid-September. The crew will outfit you in raingear if needed, provide tackle and bait, and clean and fillet your catch. **Aiden's Deep Sea Fishing** (902/963-3522, www.peifishing.com) has been in business for decades and has three excursions (adult $45, child $35) scheduled daily between mid-June and mid-September.

Accommodations and Camping

Accommodations at **Rustico Resort** (corner of Rte. 6 and Rte. 242, Rustico, 902/963-2357, www.rusticoresort.com; May-Oct.; $145-250 s or d) are usually filled with golfers, who stay in the cottages (from $210 s or d, including breakfast and unlimited golf on the adjacent 18-hole course). Other amenities include motel-style rooms, grass tennis courts, a heated pool, paddleboard rentals and lessons, and a restaurant with tasty pizzas from $14.

The 1870 **Barachois Inn** (2193 Church Rd., Rustico, 902/963-2194 or 800/963-2194, www.barachoisinn.com; May-Oct.; $165-295 s or d) overlooks Rustico Bay from just off Route 243. The main house holds four historically themed guest rooms, while the adjacent McDonald House contains four larger, more modern rooms. Rates include a full breakfast.

Cymbria Tent and Trailer Park (729 Grand Pere Point Rd., Cambria, 902/963-2458, www.cymbria.ca; June-early Sept.; tent sites $30, hookups $33-36) occupies a quiet 12-hectare location close to the beach, four kilometers east of Rustico. Facilities include a store, game room, playground, dump station, and hot showers.

Food

Fisherman's Wharf Lobster Suppers (7230 Rustico Rd., North Rustico, 902/963-2669; mid-May-mid-Oct. daily 11am-8pm) is a cavernous 500-seat restaurant that attracts the tour bus crowd from Cavendish and Charlottetown. Although it's open for lunch, the lobster supper doesn't start until 4pm. Choose from three different sizes of lobster

($32-40), pay your money, and join the fray. The cost includes one full lobster and unlimited trips to the super-long buffet counter, including chowder, mussels, hot entrées, salad, dessert, and hot drinks.

If your accommodation has cooking facilities, head to **Doiron Fisheries** (North Rustico dock, 902/963-2442; May-early Oct. daily 8am-8pm) for lobsters, mussels, clams, fish, and delicious Malpeque oysters.

Getting There

Rustico is 10 kilometers (10 minutes) west of Brackley Beach along Route 6. To get to Rustico Bay directly from Charlottetown, go north on Route 2, then west on Route 6, for a total of 30 kilometers (30 minutes).

★ NORTH RUSTICO HARBOUR

The tiny village of North Rustico Harbour, on the north side of Rustico Bay, is one of my favorite spots on Prince Edward Island. It's around 1.5 kilometers east of North Rustico by road, but a more enjoyable way to get there is to walk along the harbor-front boardwalk from North Rustico. The village itself has only a few homes, built on a slight rise sloping down to the water. At the end of the road you'll find a

restored wharf with shops and cafes, sea kayak rentals, and a few shops. Add to the scene an old wooden lighthouse, a beach that is used as a parking lot at low tide, and one of the region's best restaurants, and you have a destination as far removed from nearby commercial Cavendish as you could imagine. Although it's out of sight from the harbor, make sure to wander across the dunes behind the lighthouse to **North Rustico Beach** (which is within Prince Edward Island National Park),

North Rustico Harbour is the push-off point for kayak tours operated by **Outside Expeditions** (370 Harbourview Dr., 902/963-3366; mid-May-mid-Oct.). A 90-minute paddle around the bay is $39 per person; a three-hour trip, with the chance of seeing abundant bird life, is $59; and a six-hour trip across to Robinsons Island is $120, including lunch.

Food

A shack on the main dock has been converted to the ★ **Blue Mussel Café** (Harbourview Dr., 902/963-2152; mid-June-mid-Sept. Mon.-Thurs. 11:30am-9pm, Fri.-Sun. 11:30am-10:30pm; $15-28), where many of the tables are outside on a private corner of the wharf. The menu reads like a list of what fisherfolk haul in from local waters—salmon, haddock,

North Rustico Harbour

mackerel, oysters, mussels, and lobster—and unlike at most other island restaurants, there's not a deep fryer in sight.

Getting There

To get to North Rustico Harbour from North Rustico, go east on Harbourview Drive for two kilometers. North Rustico Harbour is about 30 kilometers (30 minutes) northwest of Charlottetown via Route 2, Route 7, and Route 6.

Cavendish

Thanks to Lucy Maud Montgomery and a certain fictional character named Anne, Cavendish, 40 kilometers northeast of Charlottetown, is Prince Edward Island's most popular tourist destination. Unfortunately, those who come here expecting to find a bucolic little oasis of tranquility will be sorely disappointed. The once rural Cavendish area has become a maze of theme parks, fast-food outlets, and souvenir shops in parts, and the village has repositioned itself as an official resort municipality to try to grapple with fame. To dedicated readers of Montgomery's sentimental books, the village's lure is emotional. For others—those who don't know Anne of Green Gables from Anne Frank—it might best be avoided. Still, if you end up here and are looking for something to do, you'll have

Cavendish and Vicinity

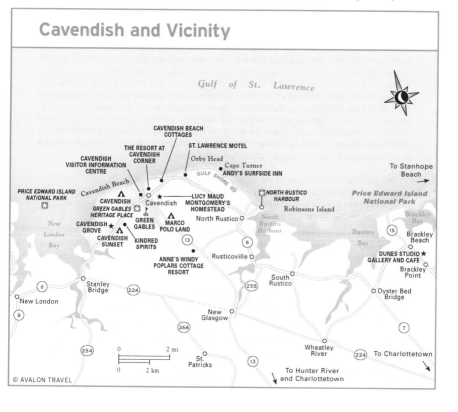

© AVALON TRAVEL

a multitude of choices—including heading into adjacent Prince Edward Island National Park, golfing at Green Gables Golf Course, or browsing through crafts shops.

Montgomery portrayed rural Cavendish as an idyllic "neverland" called Avonlea, imbued with innocence and harmony. Beyond the crass commercialism, as you drive the rambling red-clay lanes and walk the quiet woods, meadows, and gulf shore, you'll have to agree that the lady did not overstate her case. The most pastoral and historic places are preserved as part of **Prince Edward Island National Park.** Cavendish itself is home to two important Anne attractions, while others dot the surrounding countryside.

★ GREEN GABLES HERITAGE PLACE

Located on the west side of the Route 6 and Route 13 intersection, **Green Gables Heritage Place** (902/963-7874; May-Oct. daily 9am-5pm; adult $8, senior $7, child $4) reigns as the idyllic hub of a Montgomery sightseeing circuit. The restored 19th-century farmhouse, once home to Montgomery's

Lucy Maud Montgomery

Lucy Maud Montgomery, known and beloved around the world as the creator of *Anne of Green Gables*, was born at New London, Prince Edward Island, in 1874, a decade after the Charlottetown Conference. When she was only two, her mother died and her father moved to western Canada. Maud, as she preferred to be called, was left in the care of her maternal grandparents, who brought her to Cavendish.

Cavendish, in northern Queens County, was idyllic in those days, and Montgomery wrote fondly about the ornate Victorian sweetness of the setting of her early years. As a young woman, she studied first at the island's Prince of Wales College and later at Dalhousie University in Halifax. She then returned to the island as a teacher at Bideford, Lower Bedeque, Belmont, and Lot 15. In 1898, her grandfather's death brought her back to Cavendish to help her grandmother.

The idea for *Anne of Green Gables* dated to her second Cavendish stay, and the book was published in 1908. In 1911, Montgomery married the Reverend Ewen MacDonald at her Campbell relatives' Silver Bush homestead overlooking the Lake of Shining Waters. (The Campbell descendants still live in the pretty farmhouse and have turned their home into a museum.) The couple moved to Ontario, where Montgomery spent the rest of her life, returning to PEI only for short visits. But Maud never forgot Prince Edward Island. Those brief revisitations with her beloved island must have been painful; after one trip, she wistfully recalled in her journal:

This evening I spent in Lover's Lane. How beautiful it was—green and alluring and beckoning! I had been tired and discouraged and sick at heart before I went to it—and it rested me and cheered me and stole away the heartsickness, giving peace and newness of life.

Montgomery died in 1942 and was buried in Cavendish Cemetery. She left 20 juvenile books and myriad other writings. Her works have been published worldwide, translated into 16 languages. In Japan, Montgomery's writings are required reading in the school system, which accounts for the island's many Japanese visitors.

Montgomery wrote for children, and she viewed Cavendish and Prince Edward Island with all the clarity and innocence that a child possesses. Her books are as timeless today as they were decades ago. Some critics have described Montgomery's writings as mawkish. Contemporary scholars, however, have taken a new look at the author's works and have begun to discern a far more complex style. The academic community may debate her literary prowess, but no matter—the honest essence of Montgomery's writings has inspired decades of zealous pilgrims to pay their respects to her native Cavendish. To islanders, she is Lucy Maud, their literary genius, on a first-name basis.

Green Gables Heritage Place

elderly cousins and the setting for her most famous book, *Anne of Green Gables,* is furnished simply and stolidly, just as it was described in the novel. A fire in 1997 badly damaged portions of the house, but repairs commenced immediately, and within a couple of weeks the landmark was back in perfect condition. Among other memorabilia in the pretty vintage setting are artifacts such as the author's archaic typewriter, on which she composed many well-loved passages. Period-style gardens, farm buildings, and an interpretive center and gift shop complete the complex. From the grounds, the Balsam Hollow and Haunted Woods trails feature some of Montgomery's favorite woodland haunts, including Lover's Lane.

LUCY MAUD MONTGOMERY HOMESTEAD

Montgomery spent much of her childhood living with her grandparents in a small home one kilometer east of Green Gables Heritage Place. "I wrote it in the evenings after my regular day's work was done," she recalled of her most famous novel, "wrote most of it at the window of the little gable room that had been mine for many years." While the main building is long gone, the stone cellar remains. Surrounded by a white picket fence and by apple trees, it has been converted to a **small museum and bookstore** (Rte. 6, 902/963-2231; mid-May-mid-Oct. daily 9am-5pm, July-Aug. daily 9am-6pm; adult $3, child $1) operated by Montgomery's descendants, who live at the end of the road.

Montgomery is buried in the nearby **Cavendish Cemetery,** at the corner of Route 6 and Route 13.

RECREATION

The focus of most visitors to Cavendish are the beaches of **Prince Edward Island National Park,** which parallel the main highway through town and are within easy walking and biking distance of many accommodations. In the heart of the commercial strip, **Cavendish Grove** was once the site of a fun park, but upon its closing, the land was incorporated into the national park. Today, it's a pleasant green space with artificial ponds, manicured lawns, and paths leading to the beach.

Golf

Little known outside Canada, Stanley Thompson was one of the world's great 20th-century golf course architects. His best-known courses are those within the country's national park system. Green Gables Golf Course (Rte. 6, 902/963-4653) may not be as revered as Thompson-designed Highland Links (Cape Breton Highlands National Park) or Banff Springs (Banff National Park), but this old-fashioned layout within Prince Edward Island National Park is a gem of composition defined by water views and deep bunkers. Regular greens fees are $100 including a cart, or pay $55 after 3pm.

Amusement Parks and Museums

The only theme park with any relationship to Anne of Green Gables is Avonlea Village (Rte. 6, 902/963-3050, http://avonlea.ca; mid-June-mid-Sept. daily 10am-5pm; adult $20, senior $18, child $16). Staff in period costumes bring Anne's world to life in musical shows that take place throughout the sprawling grounds. Visitors are invited to try their hand at milking a cow, learn how to barn dance, and tour an old-fashioned chocolate factory.

You'll see the rides of Sandspit Amusement Park (8986 Cavendish Rd., 902/963-3939, www.sandspit.com; last two weeks of June daily 10am-6pm, July-Aug. daily 10am-10pm), east of the junction of Routes 6 and 13, long before arriving at the front gate. The huge park, a magnet for kids on vacation, features a roller coaster (The Cyclone, billed as the largest in the Maritimes), a carousel, and other rides, rides, rides. It's free to get in, but each ride costs a small amount. All-day ride packages cost $13-25, depending on your height.

And what tourist town would be complete without a Ripley's Believe It or Not! Museum (Rte. 6, 902/963-2242; June and Sept. daily 9:30am-5pm, July-Aug. daily 9am-8pm; adult $13, senior $10, child $7) or a wax museum—in this case, the adjacent Wax World of the Stars (Rte. 6, 902/963-3444; early June-early Sept. 10am-4:30pm, July-Aug. 9am-7:30pm; adult $13, senior $10, child $7), which is exactly as the name suggests.

Green Gables Golf Course

ACCOMMODATIONS AND CAMPING

While accommodations in Cavendish are plentiful, they book up well in advance for July and August. No place in Atlantic Canada sees a more dramatic drop in room rates for the shoulder seasons (mid-May-June and Sept.-mid-Oct.), while the rest of the year, most accommodations close completely.

Under $50

★ **Andy's Surfside Inn** (Gulf Shore Rd., 902/963-2405; June-Nov.; $55-85 s or d) is a big old whitewashed home right on the ocean, a few kilometers east of Cavendish along the coastal road. The rooms and facilities are older, but the setting can't be beat. Only one room has its own bathroom; other amenities include a deck, bikes, and a barbecue.

$50-100

The **St. Lawrence Motel** (351 Gulf Shore Rd., 902/963-2053 or 800/387-2053, www.stlawrencemotel.com; mid-May-early Oct.; $78-173 s or d) is within Prince Edward Island National Park between Cavendish and North Rustico. Set on eight hectares, this 16-room property overlooks the gulf, a short walk from the water. All but one of the units has a kitchen, and the largest have three bedrooms. The beach is a short walk down the road, and on-site amenities include an outdoor swimming pool, a recreation room, barbecues, and lawn games such as horseshoes and croquet. Rates include a pass for national park entry.

Silverwood Motel (Rte. 6, 902/963-2439 or 800/565-4753, www.silverwoodmotel.com; June-Sept.; $89-149 s or d) has regular motel rooms as well as one- and two-bedroom units with kitchens. There's also a pool and adjacent restaurant.

Over $100

The Resort at Cavendish Corner (corner of Rte. 6 and Rte. 13, 902/963-2251 or 877/963-2251, www.resortatcavendishcorner.com; May-Oct.; $108-300 s or d) offers more than 100 rooms and cottages spread across a three-hectare site, across from the main visitor center and within walking distance of the beach. Amenities include barbecues, two outdoor heated pools, two playgrounds, a restaurant, and wireless Internet throughout.

From ★ **Kindred Spirits Country Inn and Cottages** (Memory Ln., off Rte. 6, 902/963-2434 or 800/461-1755, www.kindredspirits.ca; mid-May-mid-Oct.; $135-375 s or d), guests can stroll along Lover's Lane to Green Gables Heritage Place, just the way Lucy Maud Montgomery described in *Anne of Green Gables*. This grandly Victorian estate is handy to the golf course as well, but it's also very private and far removed from busy Route 6. Bed-and-breakfast rooms in the main inn ($135-180 s or d) are decorated with stylish antiques. Some have balconies and fireplaces. Surrounding the inn are 14 kitchen-equipped cottages, each surrounded by green space. Rates range from $205 for a one-bedroom unit to $375 for a three-bedroom cottage with a whirlpool bath.

Overlooking the Gulf of St. Lawrence from within Prince Edward Island National Park is **Cavendish Beach Cottages** (1445 Gulf Shore Rd., 902/963-2025, www.cavendishbeachcottages.com; early May-Sept.; $165-219 s or d), a complex of 13 simply furnished yet modern cottages, each with a deck offering ocean views. The cottages, set back 200 meters from the beach, are just a few steps from the park's jogging and hiking trails. Off-season rates (May and Sept.) start at $120.

The price may seem a little high considering its location more than two kilometers from the beach, but **Anne's Windy Poplars Cottage Resort** (Rte. 1, 902/963-2888 or 800/363-5888, www.anneswindypoplars.com; late Apr.-mid-Oct.; $200-380 s or d) has many things going for it—spacious and immaculate cottages, a pleasant pool complex with a hot tub and sauna, and well-tended gardens dotted with playgrounds. The cottages all come with kitchens, decks, up to three bedrooms, and wireless Internet.

Kindred Spirits Country Inn and Cottages

Campgrounds

What ★ Cavendish Campground (late May-early Oct.; $28-36) lacks in facilities it makes up for in location, close to the ocean within Prince Edward Island National Park and just a few kilometers from downtown Cavendish. Amenities include showers, kitchen shelters, and fire pits (firewood $8 per bundle). Even with more than 300 campsites, it fills most summer days, so plan on arriving before noon or booking a site in advance. These can be made through the Parks Canada Campground Reservation Service (877/737-3783, www.pccamping.ca) for $11 per reservation.

Marco Polo Land (Rte. 13, 902/963-2352 or 800/665-2352, www.marcopololand.com; late May-mid-Sept.; $32.50-43) is the island's definitive commercial campground, replete with resort trappings. Facilities at the 40-hectare park include more than 400 campsites ($24-31), tennis courts, mini-golf, a full-sized outdoor pool, a street hockey rink, a petting zoo, a wading pool, a restaurant, and a grocery store.

The 465-site Sunset Campground (Rte. 6, 902/963-2440 or 800/715-2440, www.campingpei.ca; late June-early Sept.; $34.50-45) is big, bold, and very family-friendly. It has many of the same amenities as Marco Polo Land, although on a smaller scale. Its selling point is its location within walking distance of Cavendish's many commercial attractions.

FOOD
Lobster Supper

Lobster suppers are casual good-value gatherings held across the island. They can be very commercial or simply an annual gathering of locals in a church basement. A great compromise is the ★ New Glasgow Lobster Suppers (Rte. 258, 902/964-2870; June-mid-Oct. 4-8:30pm), eight kilometers southeast of Cavendish along Route 13. In operation since 1958, this one fills a cavernous hall with up to 500 diners at a time. It even has its own lobster holding pond, allowing the tradition to continue beyond lobster fishing season. Choose the size of lobster and pay at the front desk, then feast on limitless mussels, clam chowder, salad, and breads until your lobster is brought to your table. Options range from a one-pound lobster ($32) to a four pounder ($65), or share a four-pound lobster for $85. If lobster isn't your thing, many other options are offered, ranging from vegetarian to scallops ($21-30).

Other Dining Options

Man cannot live on lobster alone, so if you're in town more than one night, you'll need to find somewhere else to eat. Iif you have cooking facilities at your accommodation (even just a barbecue), pick up fresh seafood at Doiron Fisheries (North Rustico dock, 902/963-2442; May-early Oct. daily 8am-8pm).

For do-it-yourself meals, take your choice of markets along major highways; shops at Cavendish Beach Shopping Plaza answer most needs. The main excuse to stop at Cavendish Boardwalk, another mall, is for an ice cream at Cow's (9139 Route 6, 902/963-2692; mid-June-mid-Sept. daily 10am-6pm).

INFORMATION AND SERVICES

Cavendish has no downtown. Instead, services such as restaurants and gas stations are scattered along a five-kilometer stretch of Route 6 southeast from the junction with Route 13. Plan on doing chores such as grocery shopping, banking, and posting mail back in Charlottetown.

Cavendish Visitor Information Centre (902/963-2391; mid-May-mid-Oct. daily 9am-5pm, July-Aug. daily 8am-9pm) is combined with the provincial Visitor Information Centre, 50 meters north of the Route 6 and Route 13 intersection, and represents local operators and accommodations. Tourism Prince Edward Island shares the building with Parks Canada (902/963-2391), which hands out national park information.

GETTING THERE

From North Rustico Harbour, it's about 15 kilometers (10 minutes) northwest to Cavendish via Route 6. To get to Cavendish directly from Charlottetown, go north on Route 2 and Route 13. The trip is about 40 kilometers (40 minutes).

VICINITY OF CAVENDISH

Hamlets encircle Cavendish. The rural scenery is lovely, and exploring the beaches and back roads should help you sharpen your appetite for a night at one of PEI's famed lobster-supper community halls, which are scattered hereabouts.

Stanley Bridge

For seaworthy sightseeing, check out Stanley Bridge Marine Aquarium (32 Campbellton Rd., 902/886-3355; mid-June-early Oct. daily 9:30am-8pm; adult $9, child $7), five kilometers southwest of Cavendish. The privately operated aquarium has native fish species in viewing tanks and exhibits on natural history and oyster cultivation; seals are kept outside in penned pools. Part of the complex is a café with a waterfront deck.

In the vicinity, shoppers like the Stanley Bridge Studios (Rte. 6, 902/886-2800; daily 10am-5pm), where shelves and floor space overflow with woolen sweaters, quilts, apparel, stoneware, porcelain, jewelry, and Anne dolls.

GETTING THERE

It's seven kilometers to Stanley Bridge from Cavendish west along Route 6. From Charlottetown, take Route 2 west then Route 230 north, then 254 north, for a total distance of 45 kilometers (50 minutes).

New London

The Lucy Maud Montgomery Birthplace (corner of Rte. 6 and Rte. 20, 902/886-2099; mid-May-mid-Oct. daily 9am-5pm; adult $4, child $2) lies 10 minutes from Cavendish, at what was once Clifton. The author was born in the unassuming house in 1874. The exhibits include her wedding dress, scrapbooks, and other personal items.

Old-fashioned tearooms dot the countryside around Cavendish, and none are more welcoming than ★ Blue Winds Tea

the Lucy Maud Montgomery Birthplace

House (10746 New London Rd., 902/886-2860; mid-May-mid-Oct. Fri.-Wed. 11:30am-5pm, Thurs. 2pm-5pm), on the south side of the village. Here, the soups are made from scratch, breads and pastries are baked daily, and recipes for treats such as New Moon Pudding are taken from historic cookbooks. On Thursday, afternoon tea is served for $14 per person.

GETTING THERE

New London is about 12 kilometers west of Cavendish via Route 6. From Charlottetown, take Route 2 west then Route 8 north, a total distance of 45 kilometers (50 minutes).

Park Corner

Anne of Green Gables Museum (Rte. 20, 902/436-7329; May-Oct. daily 11am-4pm, summer daily 9am-5pm; adult $5, child $2), eight kilometers northwest of New London, is another Montgomery landmark and the ancestral home of the author's Campbell relatives. The estate spreads out in a farmhouse setting in the pastoral rolling countryside, with the Lake of Shining Waters, described in *Anne of Green Gables,* in front of the main buildings. Montgomery described the house as "the big beautiful home that was the wonder castle of my dreams," and here she was married in 1911. The museum's exhibits include Montgomery's personal correspondence and first editions of her works.

GETTING THERE

Park Corner is 22 kilometers (25 minutes) northwest of Cavendish. Get there by taking Route 6 west, then Route 20 north. The village is 70 kilometers (one hour) northwest of Charlottetown via Routes 2, 8, and 20.

Prince County

Look for ★ to find recommended sights, activities, dining, and lodging.

Highlights

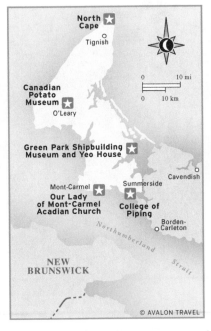

★ **College of Piping:** Students from around the world gather at this school to learn the art of bagpiping and Highland dancing. Visitors are more than welcome to watch (page 44).

★ **Green Park Shipbuilding Museum and Yeo House:** An attraction that is as scenic as it is historic, this waterfront estate was once the center of a thriving shipbuilding industry (page 48).

★ **Our Lady of Mont-Carmel Acadian Church:** This magnificent church rises high above the trim Acadian homes of Mont-Carmel (page 50).

★ **Canadian Potato Museum:** Learn about the province's main agricultural crop at this museum; it is more interesting than the name might suggest (page 52).

★ **North Cape:** Drive to the end of the road on Prince Edward Island and you'll find yourself in the middle of a wind farm with panoramic ocean views in all directions (page 56).

Prince County encompasses the western third of Prince Edward Island. Like Kings County in the east, it is well off the main tourist path. Along the southern portion of Prince County, the land is level, and the pastoral farmlands flow in gentle serene sweeps to the strait coastline. Thick woodlands span the county's midsection, and you'll see fields of potatoes that blossom in July and green carpets of wheat nodding in the summer breezes. The northern tip is a remote and barren plain with a windswept coast, where farmers known as "mossers" use stout draft horses to reap Irish moss (a seaweed) from the surf.

Summerside, the province's second-largest town, boasts an ample supply of lodgings, restaurants, and nightlife. Just west of there is the province's largest Acadian area, the Région Évangéline. Count on high-quality crafts and wares at town boutiques and outlying shops throughout the region; the region's craftspeople are renowned for quilts, knitted apparel, Acadian shirts, and blankets.

Route 2, PEI's main expressway, enters Prince County at the town of Kensington, glides past the seaport of Summerside on a narrow isthmus, and leads inland for 100 kilometers to finish at the village of Tignish, near the island's northwestern tip. The highways up and down the east and west coasts come together as Lady Slipper Scenic Drive, one of the provincial scenic sightseeing routes (it's signposted with a red symbol of the orchidlike flower). The county's most idyllic scenery—and some of the island's most spectacular sea views—lie along this route, at the sea's edges of Northumberland Strait and the Gulf of St. Lawrence. About 50 meandering side roads lead off the coastal route to connect with Route 2 and others. You may become temporarily lost on the roads, but not for long—the blue sea invariably looms around the next bend.

PLANNING YOUR TIME

It's possible to reach the northern tip of Prince County on a day trip from Charlottetown, but a more sensible option if you have just one day would be to concentrate on the southern half of

---

Previous: Summerside Harbour; Jacques Cartier Provincial Park. **Above:** the Acadian flag painted on a rock in Region Evangeline.

Prince County

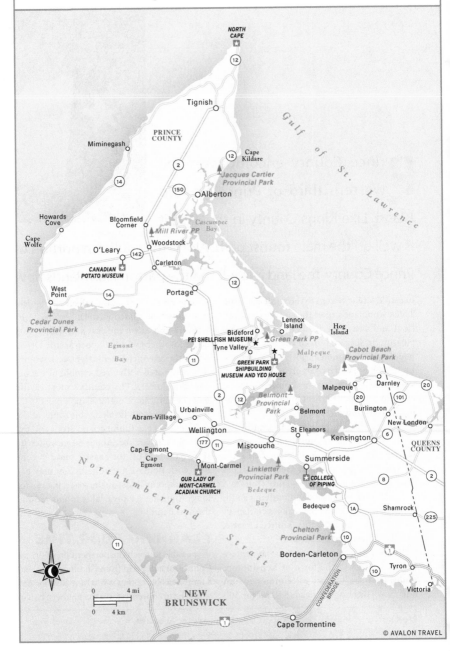

© AVALON TRAVEL

the county. A suggested route would be to stop in Summerside to visit the **College of Piping,** drive through Région Évangéline past the spectacular **Our Lady of Mont-Carmel Acadian Church,** and jog north to the **Green Park Shipbuilding Museum and Yeo House.** The main reason to explore further is for the coastal scenery, especially along the Northumberland Strait. Other attractions include the **Canadian** **Potato Museum,** golfing at Mill River, and the feeling of accomplishment of driving to the end of the road at **North Cape.**

Tourist services are more limited in Prince County than elsewhere in the province. You should be able to find somewhere to stay with a few days' notice, but for top picks such as **West Point Lighthouse** (West Point), plan on being disappointed if you arrive without reservations.

Summerside

Summerside (pop. 16,500), 60 kilometers west of Charlottetown and 30 kilometers northwest of the Confederation Bridge, is Prince Edward Island's second-largest town and its main shipping port. It's got all the bustle yet none of the seaminess usually associated with seaports. Stately old homes anchor wide lawns, and quiet streets are edged with verdant canopies.

SIGHTS AND RECREATION
Along the Harbor

The tourist's Summerside lies along Heather Moyse Drive, where **Spinnakers' Landing** was developed after a military base was phased out. The complex comprises numerous shops and restaurants, an outdoor stage

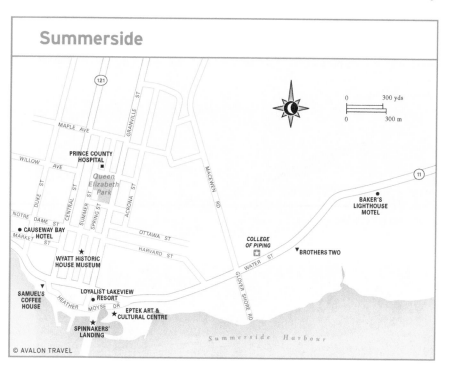

© AVALON TRAVEL

built over the water, a nautical-themed playground, and a lighthouse.

Taking its name from the Mi'kmaq word for "hot spot," **Eptek Art & Cultural Centre** (130 Heather Moyse Dr., 902/888-8373; July-Aug. Mon.-Sat. 9am-5pm, Sun. noon-5pm, the rest of the year Tues.-Fri. 10am-4pm; admission varies) has a spacious main gallery hosting touring national fine arts and historical exhibits.

Wyatt House Museum

The home of Wanda Lefurgey Wyatt until her death at 102 in 1998, the grandly restored **Wyatt House Museum** (85 Spring St., 902/432-1327; July-Aug. Mon.-Sat. 10am-5pm; adult $6, child $4.50) allows you to step back into the lives of a well-to-do family with long ties to the Summerside community. Adding to the charm are guided tours of the 1867 home led by costumed guides.

★ College of Piping

The **College of Piping** (619 Water St. E., 902/436-5377, www.collegeofpiping.com), affiliated with Scotland's College of Piping in Glasgow, attracts students from around the world to its teaching programs of Highland dancing, step dancing, fiddling, and bagpiping. Students perform for the public at a series of summer concerts that take place weekdays at 11:30am, 1:30pm, and 3:30pm in July and August ($5 per person). Another program open to the public is the Highland Storm ceilidh (July-Aug. Tues.-Thurs. 7pm; adult $35, senior $29, child $23).

ACCOMMODATIONS AND CAMPING

Summerside's least expensive motel is **Baker's Lighthouse Motel** (802 Water St., 902/436-2992, www.bakerslighthousemotel. com; $65 s, $75-85 d), two kilometers east of downtown. The rooms are plain but clean and comfortable. There's also wireless Internet access and air-conditioning.

The 108-room **Causeway Bay Hotel** (311 Market St., 902/436-2157 or 800/565-7829, www.causewaybayhotels.ca; $135-195) is centrally located and offers large rooms (some with kitchenettes), an indoor pool, a restaurant, a lounge, and amenities for the physically challenged.

Across the road from Spinnakers' Landing, **Loyalist Lakeview Resort** (195 Heather

Spinnakers' Landing

Moyse Dr., 902/436-3333 or 877/355-3500, www.lakeviewhotels.com; $155-205 s or d) features 103 spacious motel rooms decorated with a distinct country inn-style decor. It offers a good range of amenities—tennis, an indoor pool, a fitness room, bike rentals, a pub, and a restaurant—making it a good choice for those looking for city-type accommodations.

Summerside's closest campground is in beachside **Linkletter Provincial Park,** eight kilometers west of town (Rte. 11, 902/888-8366; early June-late Sept.; $28-35). This 30-hectare park on Bedeque Bay has 84 serviced and unserviced sites, hot showers, and a launderette, dump station, kitchen shelter, and nearby store.

FOOD

At the west end of the original main street (uphill from the waterfront), **Samuel's Coffee House Two** (4 Queen St., 902/724-2300; Mon.-Thurs. 7:30am-5pm, Fri. 7:30am-9pm, Sat. 8am-4pm, Sun. 9am-4pm; lunches $6-9) pours the best coffee in town within a stylish room at street level of a historic red-brick bank building. A coffee and muffin before 9am is just $3, but the breakfast sandwiches are also good. The rest of the day, expect soups, sandwiches, and muffins, all freshly made and delicious.

Away from the water, **Brothers Two** (618 Water St. E., 902/436-9654; Sun.-Thurs. 11:30am-9pm, Fri.-Sat. 11:30am-10pm; $14-24) has been Summerside's social hub for decades. It's no-frills family-style seafood dining at its best. Mains come as simple as meatloaf and as fancy as scallops poached in white wine. If it's a warm evening, talk your way into a table on the rooftop patio.

INFORMATION

In the heart of harbor-front Spinnakers' Landing, the **Visitor Information Centre** (124 Heather Moyse Dr., 902/888-8364, www.exploresummerside.com; late June-early Sept. daily 9:30am-9:30pm) is well signposted as you come into town.

GETTING THERE

Summerside is 60 kilometers (45 minutes) west of Charlottetown via Route 2. To get to Summerside from the Confederation Bridge, take Route 10 north from Borden-Carleton, then go west on Route 11, for a total of 25 kilometers (20 minutes).

the College of Piping

Malpeque Bay

Sheltered from the open gulf by the long, narrow sandbar of Hog Island, the shallow waters of broad Malpeque Bay are tranquil and unpolluted. The bay's long fretted coastline is deserted, nearly bereft of development apart from three small provincial parks. Conditions are perfect for the large oyster fishery that thrives here. Ten million Malpeque oysters—Canada's largest source of the shellfish—are harvested each year. The purity of the bay water in part accounts for the excellent flavor of the oysters, which has made them famed worldwide as a gustatory treat. You'll find them served in a variety of ways at restaurants in the region.

KENSINGTON

Kensington lies at the intersection of five roads, including the trans-island Route 2. Summerside is 15 kilometers to the southwest, Charlottetown is 48 kilometers to the east, and Cavendish is 38 kilometers to the northeast.

Sights

Make your first stop **Kensington Railyards,** where you'll find the **Welcome Centre** (902/836-3031, www.kata.pe.ca; May-Oct. daily 9am-9pm) and a **farmers market** (July-Sept. Sat. 10am-2pm), a good place to come for fresh produce, baked goods, snacks, and crafts.

On the main road through town, **Haunted Mansion** (81 Victoria St. W., 902/836-3336; mid-June and early Sept. daily 10am-4pm, July-Aug. daily 9am-7pm; adult $13, senior $12, child $9) is a popular spot with children. This imposing Tudor-style mansion was built in the 1890s by a homesick Englishman and has been reinvented as a tourist attraction, with access included to the labyrinth of underground rooms and extensive gardens.

Getting There

Kensington is about 15 kilometers (15 minutes) northeast of Summerside via Route 2. It's 45 kilometers (40 minutes) northwest of Charlottetown via Route 2.

Haunted Mansion

CABOT BEACH PROVINCIAL PARK

From Kensington, Route 2 loops around the head of Malpeque Bay to the Tyne Valley, but Cabot Beach Provincial Park (902/836-8945; late June-early Sept.) is worth the 10-minute detour.

This 140-hectare park, 30 kilometers north of Summerside on Route 105, is the most worthwhile attraction along the east side of Malpeque Bay. It occupies a gorgeous setting on a peninsula tip just inside the bay, including a coastline of sandy beaches broken by rocky headlands. At the park's day-use area is Fanning School (mid-June-mid-Sept. daily 10am-dusk; free), a schoolhouse built in 1794 and unique (for the time) for having two stories. Finally closed in 1969, it's now open to the public. Facilities at the park campground include more than 150 sites (unserviced sites $26, hookups $32), a supervised ocean beach, a launderette, hot showers, kitchen shelters, and a nearby general store.

Getting There

Cabot Beach is 15 kilometers (15 minutes) north of Kensington via Route 20.

It's 60 kilometers (one hour) northwest of Charlottetown via Routes 2 and 20.

WEST SIDE OF MALPEQUE BAY
Tyne Valley

Quiet and bucolic, the crossroads hamlet of Tyne Valley (pop. 200), at the intersection of backcountry Routes 12, 178, and 167, lies on the west side of Malpeque Bay, a 50-minute drive from Summerside and uncountable kilometers from the rest of the modern world.

In the 1800s, Tyne Valley began as a Green Park suburb. Two generations of the Yeo family dominated the island's economy with their shipbuilding yards on Malpeque Bay, and the empire begun by James Yeo—the feisty, entrepreneurial English merchant who arrived in the 1830s—spawned the next generation's landed gentry.

The empire's riches are gone, but the lovely landscape remains, like a slice of Lucy Maud Montgomery's utopian Avonlea, transplanted from Cavendish to this corner of Prince County. To get there, follow Route 12 around Malpeque Bay, or from Route 2, turn east on Route 132 or 133. The paved and red-clay

Tyne Valley is a picturesque village on the west side of Malpeque Bay.

roads ripple across the farmlands like velvet ribbons on plump quilts.

The quiet village stirs to life in the first weekend of August with the **Tyne Valley Oyster Festival** (www.peioysterfest.com), a three-day tribute to Malpeque oysters. Daytime oyster-farming exhibits and evening oyster and lobster dinners are accompanied by talent shows, oyster-shucking demonstrations, fiddling and step-dancing contests, a parade, and a dance.

GREEN PARK PROVINCIAL PARK

Take Route 12 east from Tyne Valley and continue north through the hamlet of Port Hill to reach the beautiful **Green Park Provincial Park,** protecting a peninsula that juts into Malpeque Bay. From the end of the road (at the Shipbuilding Museum), a three-kilometer hiking trail brings you as deep into the bay as you can go without getting your feet wet. (Wear sneakers anyway, and bring insect repellent; mosquitoes flourish in the marsh pools.) The trail starts among white birches, short and stunted because of the bay's winter winds and salt. Beyond there, the path wends through hardwood groves, brightened with a ground cover of pink wild roses, bayberries, and goldenrod. Eventually the trail gives way to marshes at the peninsula's tip. The small inland ponds at the bay's edge are all that remain of a local effort to start oyster aquaculture decades ago. Marsh hay and wild grasses bend with the sea winds. Minnows streak in tidal pools, and razor clams exude continuous streams of bubbles from their invisible burrows beneath the soggy sand.

A 58-site campground (902/831-2370; late June-early Sept.; $26-32) fronts the bay beneath tree canopies on a sheltered coastal notch. It offers a launderette, kitchen shelters, hot showers, a riverside beach, and summer nature programs.

★ GREEN PARK SHIPBUILDING MUSEUM AND YEO HOUSE

The **Green Park Shipbuilding Museum and Yeo House** (902/831-7947; June Mon.-Fri. 9am-5pm, July-Aug. daily 9am-5pm; adult $5, child $3.50) lies on the edge of the provincial park. The Yeo House sits back on a sweep of verdant lawn. It's a gorgeous estate, fronted by a fence that rims the curving road. Inside, rooms are furnished with period antiques. Up four flights of stairs, the cupola—from which James Yeo would survey his shipyard—overlooks the grounds and sparkling Malpeque Bay. Behind the house,

artifacts at the Green Park Shipbuilding Museum

the museum has exhibits explaining the history and methods of wooden shipbuilding, Prince Edward Island's main industry in the 19th century. From these buildings, it's a short walk through a meadow to the water, where outdoor displays include a partially finished vessel cradled on a frame, plus historic shipbuilding equipment.

PEI SHELLFISH MUSEUM

North of Tyne Valley, turn onto Route 166 to reach the modest **PEI Shellfish Museum** (166 Bideford Rd., Bideford, 902/853-2181; late June-early Sept. Mon.-Sat. 9am-5pm, Sun. 1pm-5pm; adult $4, child $2.50). Everything you could ever want to know about oysters and mussels is explained. A small aquarium contains mollusks, lobsters, snails, and inshore fish; outside, experimental farming methods are underway in the bay.

GETTING THERE

Tyne Valley is about 45 kilometers (45 minutes) northwest of Kensington via Routes 2, 132, then 178. It's 90 kilometers (1.5 hours) northwest of Charlottetown via Routes 2, 132, then 178.

Lennox Island

A causeway off Route 163 brings you to this small island, home to 250 people of Mi'kmaq ancestry intent on cultivating oysters, spearing eels, trapping, and hunting while pursuing recognition of the 18th-century treaties with England that entitled them to their land. The province's Mi'kmaq are said to have been the first native Canadians converted to Christianity. Their history is kept alive at the **Mi'kmaq Cultural Centre** (8 Eagle Feather Trail, 902/831-2476; summer Mon.-Sat. 10am-7pm, Sun. noon-6pm; donation). The 1895 **St. Anne's Roman Catholic Church,** a sacred tribute to their patron saint, grips the island's coastline and faces the sea. A crafts shop just north of the church markets Mi'kmaq baskets, silver jewelry, pottery, and other wares.

GETTING THERE

Lennox Island is about 15 kilometers (15 minutes) northeast of Tyne Valley via Route 12 and Route 163. It's 100 kilometers (1.5 hours) northwest of Charlottetown via Routes 2, 133, 12, then 163.

Région Évangéline

The bilingual inhabitants of the Région Évangéline, the province's largest Acadian area, date their ancestry to France's earliest settlement efforts. The region offers French-flavored culture at more than a dozen villages spread west of Summerside between Route 2 and the strait seacoast. Miscouche, the commercial center, is a 10-minute drive west of Summerside on Route 2, and Mont-Carmel, the region's seaside social and tourist hub, is 30 minutes from the seaport along coastal Route 11.

MISCOUCHE

As you approach from the east, the high double spires of **St. John the Baptist Church** announce from miles away that you've left Protestant, Anglo Prince Edward Island behind and are arriving in Catholic territory.

The village of 700 inhabitants at the intersection of Routes 2 and 12 began with French farmers from Port-la-Joye in the 1720s, augmented by Acadians who fled England's Acadian deportation in 1755. The settlement commands a major historical niche among Atlantic Canada's Acadian communities and was the site of the 1884 Acadian Convention, which adopted the French tricolor flag, with the single gold star symbolizing Mary.

Musée Acadien

On the east side of town, **Musée Acadien** (Rte. 2, 902/432-2880; mid-May-mid-Oct. Mon.-Sat. 9am-5pm; adult $4.50, student

$3.50) is a genealogical resource center and also has exhibits of early photographs, papers, and artifacts, as well as a book corner (mainly in French) with volumes about Acadian history and culture since 1720. Don't miss the documentary on events leading up to the 1755 Acadian deportation; it's screened on demand.

Getting There

Miscouche is 20 kilometers west of Kensington via Route 2, a 15-minute drive. It's 65 kilometers (one hour) west of Charlottetown, also via Route 2.

MONT-CARMEL

Two kilometers south of Miscouche and 24 kilometers west of Summerside, the backcountry Route 12 meets the coastal Route 11 (Lady Slipper Drive), which lopes south and west across Acadian farmlands to this hamlet, best known for Le Village, a complex of lodgings with a restaurant. Mont-Carmel, 16 kilometers from Miscouche, makes a handy sightseeing base for touring the Région Évangéline.

★ Our Lady of Mont-Carmel Acadian Church

The magnificent **Our Lady of Mont-Carmel Acadian Church,** between Route 11 and the red cliffs fronting Northumberland Strait, reflects the cathedral style of France's Poitou region, which is renowned for its Romanesque churches featuring elaborate exteriors. The cathedral is open Sunday during Mass. For permission to enter at other times, ask at the **Musée Religieux** (902/854-2260; July-Aug. daily 1pm-5pm; donation), across the road.

Getting There

Mont-Carmel is 25 kilometers west of Summerside. It's a 30-minute drive along Route 11. Head west from Charlottetown to Summerside on Route 2, then west on Route 11, for a total distance of 85 kilometers (1.5 hours).

Our Lady of Mont-Carmel Acadian Church

CONTINUING ALONG ROUTE 11
Cap-Egmont

A few kilometers west of Mont-Carmel is the village of Cap-Egmont, best known for the very un-Acadian **Bottle Houses** (Rte. 11, 902/854-2987; mid-May-early Oct. daily 9am-6pm, July-Aug. 9am-8pm; adult $6.50, senior $6, child $2). They are the work of Edouard Arsenault, who in the 1970s mortared together 25,000 glass bottles of all colors, shapes, and sizes to form three astonishing buildings—a chapel with an altar and pews, a tavern, and a six-gabled house. The structures qualified for inclusion in *Ripley's Believe It or Not.*

Turn off on the west side of the village to reach **Cape Egmont Lighthouse.** Although it's not open to the public, this light sits in a commanding position overlooking Northumberland Strait. Built in 1884, it is the same design as the one at Wood Islands (where the ferry from Nova Scotia docks), and

Cape Egmont Lighthouse

like other lighthouses around the island, it has been moved back from the ocean edge as erosion has taken its toll on surrounding cliffs.

GETTING THERE

Cap-Egmont is about five kilometers west of Mont-Carmel via Route 11. From Charlottetown, head west on Route 2 to Summerside, then west on Route 11, for a total distance of 90 kilometers (1.5 hours).

Abram-Village

From Cap-Egmont, the scenic coastal Route 11 wends north for 10 kilometers and turns inland to this hamlet known for crafts. **La Co-op d'Artisanat d'Abram Village** (Abram's Village Handcraft Co-op, 2181 Cannontown Rd., 902/854-2096; mid-June-mid-Sept. Mon.-Sat. 9:30am-5pm), at the intersection of Routes 11 and 124 is the area's definitive crafts source, with weavings, rugs, Acadian shirts, pottery, and dolls.

GETTING THERE

To get to Abram-Village from Mont-Carmel, take Route 11 west, then north, for a total of 15 kilometers (15 minutes). From Charlottetown, it's 90 kilometers (1.5 hours) west on Routes 2 and 124.

Western Prince County

Beyond Summerside and the Région Évangéline, Route 2 cuts into the interior, out of sight of the seas. Nonetheless, most backcountry roads off the main route eventually finish at the water. To the west, the Northumberland Strait is the pussycat of summer seas, and the warm surf laps peacefully along the southern and western coastlines. The Gulf of St. Lawrence, however, is more temperamental, with a welter of rolling waves breaking onto the north shore.

For sightseeing information, stop at the provincial **Visitor Information Centre** in Portage (Rte. 2, 902/831-7930; July-Aug. daily 9am-7pm, June and Sept. daily 9am-4:30pm), which is 43 kilometers north of Summerside.

MILL RIVER PROVINCIAL PARK

As you exit Route 2 at Woodstock, you enter a wooded realm on a ribbon of a road into **Mill River Provincial Park.** The park meshes lush landscapes with contemporary resort trappings and full recreation facilities, including the championship-quality Mill River Golf Course.

Recreation

The 18-hole, par-72 **Mill River Golf Course** (902/859-8873 or 800/377-8339) is generally regarded as one of Canada's top 100 courses and has hosted many national events through the years. The course spans 6,747 yards and is open May through October. During July and August, you'd be wise to make reservations 48 hours in advance. Greens fees range $70-85.

On warmer days, **Mill River Fun Park** (902/859-3915; July-Aug. daily 11am-7pm; $9 per person, child under 6 free), offering waterslides and outdoor pools, is a good place for families looking for watery fun.

Accommodations and Food

The three-story **Rodd Mill River** (Rte. 2, 902/859-3555 or 800/565-7633, www.roddvacations.com; Jan.-Oct.; $155-295 s or d) is a sleek wood-sided hotel with 90 spacious and modern rooms and suites. Guests are attracted to the resort-style activities—golf, tennis, canoeing, swimming, and more. The resort's **Hernewood Dining Room** boasts regionally renowned dining that draws an appreciative clientele from Summerside; expect a reasonably priced menu ($21-27 for a dinner main) featuring seafood specialties, with a dish-of-the-day emphasis on salmon, halibut, or lobster.

The park's riverfront campground (902/859-8790; mid-June-late Sept.) has 72 sites: 18 unserviced ($28), 18 with two-way hookups ($32), and 36 with full hookups ($35). Amenities include kitchen shelters, hot showers, a launderette, and summer interpretive programs.

Getting There

Mill River Provincial Park is 60 kilometers (50 minutes) northwest of Summerside along Route 2. It's 120 kilometers (1.5 hours) northwest of Charlottetown via Route 2.

O'LEARY

On Prince Edward Island, O'Leary is synonymous with potatoes. Legend has it that the hamlet took its name from an Irish farmer who settled here in the 1830s. By 1872, rail service connected the hamlet with the rest of the island, and with that link in place, O'Leary was on its way to becoming Canada's largest potato producer.

O'Leary straddles backcountry Route 142, a five-minute drive from Route 2 and 50 minutes from Summerside. You might expect mountains of potatoes; rather, O'Leary (pop. 900) is a tidy place, nestled in the midst of surprisingly attractive fields of low-growing potato plants. If you're in the area during the autumn harvest, you'll see the fields lighted by tractor headlights as the farmers work late at night to harvest the valuable crop before the frost.

★ Canadian Potato Museum

Don't be put off by the name; the **Canadian Potato Museum** (1 Dewar Ln., off Rte. 142, 902/859-2039; mid-May-mid-Oct. Mon.-Sat. 9am-5pm, Sun. 1pm-5pm; adult $8, senior $7, family $18) is an interesting stop that depicts the history of Prince Edward Island's most famous crop. The museum explains the story of the potato's humble beginnings in South America, the way the crop is grown and harvested, and how science has played a hand in the potatoes we eat today. A barn, a schoolhouse, and a chapel are out back. Within the museum is the **Tater Kitchen** (mid-May-mid-Oct. Mon.-Sat. 11am-3pm, Sun. 1pm-4pm), with rotating daily specials such as potato oyster stew and cottage pie. You can order a loaded potato, potato soup, and poutine (fries topped with gravy and cheese curds). Save room for a slice of seaweed pie, which is actually a slice of cake made with locally harvested seaweed and topped with strawberry sauce and whipped cream.

Getting There

O'Leary is 60 kilometers (50 minutes) northwest of Summerside via Routes 2 and 142. It's 120 kilometers (1.5 hours) northwest of Charlottetown via Routes 2 and 142.

WEST POINT AND VICINITY

Route 14 exits Route 2 at Carleton, eight kilometers west of Portage, doglegs west across the verdant farmlands, and heads to West Point at the island's western tip. From there, the scenic coastal route hugs the strait shore and brings some of the island's most magnificent sea views—a total distance of 80 kilometers to Tignish. Potato fields peter out at the strait coastline, which is definitely off the beaten tourist route. The coast's long stretches of beach are interspersed with craggy red cliffs.

Cedar Dunes Provincial Park

Cedar Dunes Provincial Park fronts Northumberland Strait 30 kilometers from Route 2. It's only a small park, but it has a sandy beach backed by sand dunes and a small campground (902/859-8785; late June-early Sept.; $28-32) with around 60 campsites, a supervised beach, an activities program, a nature trail, kitchen shelters, a nearby store, and hot showers.

Within the park is one-of-a-kind ★ West Point Lighthouse (Cedar Dunes Park Rd., 902/859-3605, www.westpointharmoney.ca; mid-June-mid-Sept.; $150-170 s or d), the only place in Canada where you can stay overnight in a lighthouse. There's just one guest room in the actual lighthouse ($170 s

or d), but others are spread through adjacent buildings. The complex also has a small museum and a gift shop.

West Point to Miminegash

Beyond West Point, Route 14 cleaves to the coastline and heads north, first to Cape Wolfe (where British General James Wolfe is said to have stepped ashore on the way to battle the French in 1759) and then to Howards Cove, fronted with precipitous cliffs of burnished red. The distance from West Point to Miminegash is 36 kilometers.

Getting There

To get to West Point from Summerside, take Route 2 west and north, then Route 14 west, for a total of 75 kilometers (just over an hour). To get there from Charlottetown, take Route 2 west and north and then Route 14 west for 135 kilometers (1.5 hours).

MIMINEGASH

Nestled beside a body of water protected from the winds of Northumberland Strait by low dunes, Miminegash is renowned as the home

Canadian Potato Museum

of people who earn a living from collecting seaweed. Storm winds whip the sea on this side of the island into a frenzy, churning sea-floor plants into a webbed fabric that floats to the surface and washes to shore. This seaweed, known as Irish moss, was traditionally used as a stabilizer in ice cream and toothpaste (a practice that continues, though to a much smaller degree than in years gone past). It is harvested from the sea by boat, as well as from along the shore—after a storm you may see locals raking the beach north of the harbor, reaping the Irish moss and hauling it away with the help of draft horses.

Getting There

Miminegash is 35 kilometers (40 minutes) north of West Point via Route 14. To get to Miminegash from Charlottetown, head west then north on Route 2, northwest on Route 145, then north on Route 14. Total driving time for this 140-kilometer trip is 1.5 hours.

ROUTE 12 NORTH TO TIGNISH

None of the three highways that lead north through Prince County to Tignish are particularly busy, but Route 12, along the Gulf of St. Lawrence, is the least traveled. It branches off Route 2 just beyond the village of Portage, 42 kilometers from Summerside.

Alberton

The seaport of Alberton (pop. 1,200) is the northern area's largest town. Named for Albert, Prince of Wales, the town began in 1820 with 40 families who worked at the shipyards in nearby Northport. Deep-sea fishing aficionados will readily find charter boats here. The Alberton Museum (457 Church St., 902/853-4048; June-Sept. Mon.-Sat. 10am-5:30pm, Sun. 1pm-5pm; donation) is in a historic stone building that was originally a courthouse and jail. Exhibits delve into the town's history with antiques, clothing, and farm tools. The fox farming display is particularly interesting.

On the south side of Alberton, Travellers Inn (Rte. 12, 902/853-2215 or 800/268-7829, www.travellersinnpei.com; $95 s or d) has average motel trappings with 14 regular motel rooms and 13 kitchen-equipped units ($85-155), an indoor heated pool, a hot tub, and a pleasant atmosphere. The motel's restaurant serves basic beef and seafood dishes.

JACQUES CARTIER PROVINCIAL PARK

It's only a short hop from Alberton back to Route 2, then 16 kilometers north to Tignish, but a worthwhile detour is to continue north on Route 12 to the coastal Jacques Cartier Provincial Park (902/853-8632;

Rail to Trail

A joy for hiking and biking, the Confederation Trail spans Prince Edward Island, extending from Tignish in the west to Elmira in the east, a distance of 279 kilometers. Spur trails, including those leading to Charlottetown's downtown waterfront and the Confederation Bridge, add an additional 80 kilometers.

The trail was developed on a decommissioned rail line. The advantages of creating the trail on a rail line were twofold—there are no hilly sections, and the route passes through dozens of towns and villages. Add a base of finely crushed gravel, extensive signage, picnic tables, benches, and lookouts, and you get one of the finest opportunities for outdoor recreation in all of Atlantic Canada.

The Confederation Trail is well promoted by both the provincial tourism authority and Island Trails (www.islandtrails.ca), a nonprofit organization that manages the system. Accommodations in villages along the route provide a handy base for traversing sections of the trail or as an overnight stop for those traveling longer distances. Some, such as the Trailside Café & Inn (Mount Stewart, 902/394-3626, www.trailside.ca), have been specifically developed for trail travelers, offering beds and meals.

Jacques Cartier Provincial Park

mid-June-early Sept.; $28-32), occupying the site where explorer Cartier is believed to have stepped ashore in 1534. The campground rims the gulf. It offers a sandy beach, over 50 campsites (many with water views), hot showers, a launderette, and a summer interpretive program.

GETTING THERE

Alberton is about 65 kilometers (one hour) north of Summerside via Route 2 and Route 12. From Charlottetown, head west then north on Route 2, then take Route 150 east, for a total distance of 125 kilometers (1.5 hours).

TIGNISH AND VICINITY

Tignish (pop. 900) is simply laid out, with Church Street/Route 2 as the main street. The town is 20 minutes from Alberton, a half-hour from O'Leary, and 80 minutes from Summerside. Stories of legendary riches and the fur that created a haute-couture sensation over a century ago embellish the lore of Tignish and the northern peninsula. The world's first successful silver fox breeding began in the Tignish area in 1887. Charles Dalton—later knighted by the queen—was the innovator; he joined with Robert Oulton from New Brunswick to breed the foxes. The pelts sold for thousands of dollars in fashion salons worldwide. From 1890 to 1912, the Dalton and Oulton partnership kept a keen eye on the venture and the number of silver fox breeding pairs. As luck would have it, generosity was their downfall: Their empire fell apart when one of the partners gave a pair of the breeding foxes to a relative. The cat—the fox, that is—was out of the bag. That single pair begat innumerable descendants that were sold worldwide, and breeding became an international business.

Sights

Make your first stop the **Tignish Cultural Centre** (Maple St., 902/882-1999; mid-June-mid-Sept. daily 10am-4pm; free), which tells the natural and human history of the area, holds the usual array of tourism brochures, and offers public Internet access. Nearby, the **St. Simon and St. Jude**

Church (902/882-2049; daily 8am-7pm) is the town's stellar attraction (and the island's largest church), notable for its frescoes of the apostles and its mighty pipe organ. The organ, built by Louis Mitchell of Montréal, features 1,118 pipes, from six inches to 16 feet in length. It was installed in 1882, and until the 1950s the organ was pumped by hand.

Accommodations and Food

Right in town, an old red-brick convent has been converted to the **Tignish Heritage Inn** (Maple St., 902/882-2491, www.tignishheritageinn.ca; mid-June-mid-Oct; $100-145 s or d). The rooms are basic but adequate, and the inn has amenities such as a lounge area, a laundry, wireless Internet, and a kitchen, as well as continental breakfast. A highlight is relaxing in the extensive garden out front. The inn is set back from Route 14, the main road through town; access it from Church St. or down beside St. Simon and St. Jude Church.

M.J.'s Bakery (300 Church St., 902/882-2454; Mon.-Sat. 11am-5pm; lunches $5-8) has a small but tasty selection of sandwiches, bread baked daily, and sweet treats like blueberry pinwheels. The bakery has a small dining area, or purchase to go.

Getting There

Tignish is 85 kilometers north of Summerside via Route 2, a 70-minute drive. To get to Tignish from Alberton, it's a 20-kilometer, 20-minute drive along either Route 2 or Route 12. From Charlottetown, head west then north on Route 2 for 140 kilometers (two hours).

★ North Cape

Some 15 kilometers north of Tignish, Route 12 ends at **North Cape,** the northern tip of Prince County. The dominant artificial feature, the **Wind Energy Institute of Canada,** juts up from the windy headland

Tignish Heritage Inn

with a federal project complex that tests and evaluates wind turbines. There's no access to the main site, although interpretive panels along its fence set the scene. Better still, make time to visit the adjacent **North Cape Wind Energy Interpretive Centre** (21817 Rte. 12, 902/882-2991; May-June daily 10am-6pm, July-Aug. daily 9am-8pm, Sept.-Oct. daily 10am-6pm; adult $6, senior and child $3), which describes the science behind the wind turbines and also has a small aquarium. The center is also the starting point for the 5.5-kilometer (round-trip) **Black Marsh Nature Trail.** This easy path passes under a windmill, over marshland, and along the rugged coastline.

When you've finished exploring the cape, head back to the interpretive center, where the **Wind and Reef Restaurant** (21817 Rte. 12, 902/882-3535; May-June daily 10am-6pm, July-Aug. daily 9am-8pm, Sept.-Oct. daily 10am-6pm; lunches $9-16) has priceless views across the Gulf of St. Lawrence.

North Cape Wind Energy Interpretive Centre

Seafood dominates the menu of this casual eatery, but there's also salads and burgers.

Four kilometers before the cape, **Island's End Motel** (42 Doyle Rd., Sea Cow Pond, 902/882-3554, www.islandsendmotel.com; $75-85 s or d) overlooks the Gulf of St. Lawrence and is within walking distance of a beach.

GETTING THERE

North Cape is about 15 kilometers (15 minutes) north of Tignish along Route 12. To get there from Charlottetown, head west then north on Route 2 to Tignish, for a total of 155 kilometers (just over two hours).

Eastern Prince Edward Island

The eastern third of Prince Edward Island, much of it within Kings County, is cut off geographically from the rest of the province by the Hillsborough River. One of this region's main attractions is the lack of crowds. It has none of

the hype of Cavendish, and its activities and sights are more limited. If you're looking for sightseeing and recreation combined with natural attractions—coastal windswept peninsula beaches, seal colonies, sand dunes, and, inland, an improbable herd of provincial bison—you'll find that and more.

A two-lane highway circumnavigates the entire region, with farmland laid out on the intensely red earth on one side, and the sea and sapphire-blue sky on the other. The eastern shore, from Cardigan through to Murray Harbour, is tattered with little offshore islands and dozens of deeply indented bays and river estuaries. The southern region's climate is warm, humid, and almost tropical; islanders refer to this region as the "banana belt," and even such crops as wine grapes and tobacco thrive here. The long northern coast is nearly straight and uninterrupted, except at large St. Peter's Bay, where a tract of coast is protected as part of Prince Edward Island National Park. The northeast area is relatively remote, lightly populated and developed, and, inland, thickly wooded. As any islander will tell you, the county's northern portion is "far out"; that is, far out of sight and out of mind from mainstream Prince Edward Island. But the pastoral inland countryside is beautiful. It is cultivated in farms of corn, berries, grains, potatoes, and tobacco, and rimmed on the north by forests and tracts of provincial woodlot plantations.

PLANNING YOUR TIME

Distances throughout the eastern portion of the island are much shorter than they may first appear when poring over the provincial road map. It is possible to drive around the entire region (under 400 kilometers) in one day from Charlottetown, and you can reach Souris, in the far eastern corner, in one hour from the capital. Visitors arriving on the island by ferry land at Wood Islands. Most make a beeline for the capital, less than an

Highlights

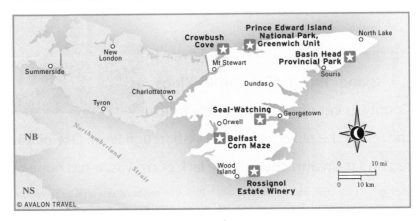

★ **Belfast Corn Maze:** If you can drag your children away from the coastline, encourage them to get lost in this country-style attraction that will keep them (hopefully) busy for hours (page 62).

★ **Rossignol Estate Winery:** Unlike the typical wine country scenery, the vineyard at Rossignol is perched atop red cliffs high above Northumberland Strait—and the wine isn't bad either (page 64).

★ **Seal-Watching:** Seal colonies inhabit islands along the southeast coast, but none are more accessible than those near Montague (page 67).

★ **Basin Head Provincial Park:** The unlikely combination of a fascinating fisheries museum and silica-filled sand that "sings" as you walk across it makes for a stop that all ages will enjoy (page 71).

★ **Prince Edward Island National Park, Greenwich Unit:** The Greenwich Unit of the island's only national park protects a moving sand dune system that is slowly burying a coastal forest (page 73).

★ **Crowbush Cove:** Prince Edward Island is dotted with golf courses, but the best is the oceanfront links at Crowbush Cove (page 74).

Eastern Prince Edward Island

Point Prim

Prince Edward Island National Park

Dunstaffnage

Gulf of St. Lawrence

To Charlottetown

Hillsborough River

Tracadie Bay

Hillsborough Bay

Gallas Point

Pownal Bay

PRINCE EDWARD ISLAND NATIONAL PARK, GREENWICH UNIT

CROWBUSH COVE

Pinette Harbour

Eldon

BELFAST CORN MAZE

Pinette

Lord Selkirk Provincial Park

Orwell Bay

Orwell

Vernon River

QUEENS COUNTY

Mount Stewart

Savage Harbour

St. Peters Bay

313

PRINCE EDWARD ISLAND NATIONAL PARK, GREENWICH UNIT

WOOD ISLANDS LIGHTHOUSE

Wood Islands

23

Olona

Montague River

KINGS COUNTY

Morell

Southampton

313

St. Peters

4

Northumberland Provincial Park

Caledonia

315

Pooles Corner

Montague

Cardigan

22

313

Monticello

16

Murray River

Brudenell River PP

Rosneath

Dundas

4

Bay Fortune

310

Rollo Bay

ROSSIGNOL ESTATE WINERY

18

Murray Harbour

Buffaloland Provincial Park

SEAL-WATCHING

Georgetown

Georgetown Harbour

3

Cardigan Bay

311

Boughton Bay

Spry Point

House Bay

Bay Fortune

Hermanville

305

Murray Harbour North

Panmure Island

Panmure Island Provincial Park

St. Mary's Bay

Boughton Island

Bay Fortune

Souris

TOWNSHEND WOODLOT

2

Poverty Beach

Northumberland

Red Point Provincial Park

BASIN HEAD PROVINCIAL PARK

Ferry to Îles de la Madeleine, Québec

Campbells Cove Provincial Park

Elmira

16

North Lake

East Point

Strait

0   5 mi
0   5 km

© AVALON TRAVEL

hour's drive to the west (unless you have children that demand a stop at the **Belfast Corn Maze**), but this is also a good starting point for exploring the region by heading in the opposite direction to Murray Harbour and beginning the convoluted coastal route north and then west along the North Shore. Aside from exploring the provincial parks and admiring the coast-meets-farmland scenery, the three highlights of the drive are taking a **seal-watching trip** from Montague, visiting the beach and museum at **Basin Head Provincial Park**, and admiring the coastal wilderness of **Prince Edward Island National Park**.

Even though Prince Edward Island is tiny, the eastern portion of the province is well off the main tourist route. This means you will find well-priced accommodations. For this reason, it's a good place to take a break from touring. An ideal scenario would be to book a cabin for a couple of days and plan on spending time exploring the surrounding area, relaxing on the beach, strolling through the surrounding towns, golfing at one of the top-notch golf courses such as **Crowbush Cove,** or doing nothing at all. Larger villages have seafood markets, so plan on doing your own cooking, then kick back in the evening with a glass of wine from **Rossignol Estate Winery,** which you pass right near the Wood Islands ferry terminal.

Along Northumberland Strait

The TransCanada Highway (Highway 1) extends east from Charlottetown for 62 kilometers to Wood Islands. This small village is the termination point for ferries from Nova Scotia, and also the starting point for touring through Kings County.

ORWELL

The small village of Orwell, 27 kilometers east of Charlottetown, has a couple of interesting historic attractions; it is also the turnoff for those cutting across Kings County to Montague.

Sights

Orwell Corner Historic Village (98 Macphail Park Rd., 902/651-8515; July-Aug. daily 9:30am-5pm, Sept.-Oct. Mon.-Fri. 9:15am-4:45pm; adult $6, child $4.25) is a restored Scottish village representing the 1890s. Buildings include the farmhouse, general store, dressmaker's shop, blacksmith's shop, church, and barns. In summer, there's a ceilidh (Celtic music and dancing) Wednesday at 8pm.

Beyond the historic village is the **Sir Andrew MacPhail Homestead** (271 Macphail Park Rd., 902/651-2789; June-mid-Dec. daily 10am-6pm; donation), the summer home of a doctor of national renown who was involved in developing the island's potato industry. Three walking trails lead through the surrounding woods.

Getting There

Orwell is 25 kilometers (25 minutes) east of Charlottetown on Route 1.

ORWELL TO WOOD ISLANDS
Eldon
★ BELFAST CORN MAZE

When the corn reaches a height of six feet, the four-hectare **Belfast Corn Maze** (5265 Hwy. 1, Eldon, 902/659-2246; Aug. daily 10am- 7pm, Sept.-Oct. Sat.-Sun. 10am-7pm; $9) fills with children and adults trying to find their way out. Cut into a different design each year, it's one of the few such mazes in Atlantic Canada, and takes at least an hour to get through. The destination is more than a maze, with a petting zoo, a giant sand box, "corn cannons'" a jumping pillow, and a rope climbing wall adding to the appeal.

The maze is part of the family-operated **Chuck Wagon Farm Market** (July-Oct. daily 10am-7pm), where produce is picked daily for the public. In addition to locally grown fruit and vegetables, you can buy jams and preserves, treat the kids to an ice cream (if they make it out of the maze), or enjoy barbeque lunch at an outdoor table.

LORD SELKIRK PROVINCIAL PARK

Tucked on the eastern shore of Orwell Bay, an inlet off the larger Hillsborough Bay, is beachfront **Lord Selkirk Provincial Park** (142 Selkirk Park Rd., 902/659-2794; late June-early Sept.). The park, named for the Scottish leader of one of the early immigrant groups, is right off the TransCanada Highway, a stone's throw west of Eldon, 10 kilometers south of Orwell. Although the beach here isn't good for swimming, it's great for walking, beachcombing, and clam digging. The park's campground has unserviced sites ($25) and hookups ($32), a swimming pool, a nine-hole golf course, minigolf, laundry, kitchen shelters, fireplaces, and a nearby campers' store.

A naturalist program runs throughout summer, and the first weekend of August, the park is the site of the annual **Highland Games,** which include piping, dancing competitions, Scottish athletic competitions, and lobster suppers.

GETTING THERE

Eldon is nine kilometers south of Orwell along Highway 1. It's 35 kilometers southeast of Charlottetown on Route 1.

Point Prim

Point Prim Lighthouse (902/659-2768; July-Aug. daily 10am-6pm; adult $3.50, child $2) is at the end of Route 209, which peels off the TransCanada Highway and runs 10 kilometers down the long slender peninsula jutting into Hillsborough Bay. Built in 1845, it's Prince Edward Island's oldest lighthouse and Canada's only circular brick lighthouse tower. The view overlooking the strait from the octagonal lantern house at the top is gorgeous.

The **Chowder House** (2150 Point Prim Rd., 902/659-2187; July-Aug. daily 11am-8pm, first two weeks of Sept. Tues.-Sun. noon-8pm; lunches $7-14) serves fresh local clams and

Belfast Corn Maze

mussels, chowder, sandwiches, and home-made breads and pastries.

GETTING THERE
Point Prim is about 20 kilometers (20 minutes) southwest of Orwell, via Routes 1 and 209. To get there from Charlottetown head east then south on Routes 1 and 209, for a total distance of 45 kilometers (45 minutes).

WOOD ISLANDS
Not an archipelago of islands at all, but a little village 60 kilometers east of the capital, this is where the ferry service from Nova Scotia unloads its cargo of vehicles and people.

Along the main highway through town is the Plough the Waves Centre (13056 Shore Rd., 902/962-3761; mid-May-mid-Oct. daily 9am-6pm), which holds the local information center.

Wood Islands Lighthouse
Ferry travelers will spot the traditional red-and-white Wood Islands Lighthouse (173 Lighthouse Rd., 902/962-3110; early June-late Sept. daily 9:30am-6pm; adult $6, senior $5, child $3) long before arriving at Wood Islands (stand on the starboard side for the best views). Dating to 1876, it is part of a small provincial park right beside the ferry dock. You can climb to the top of the lighthouse and admire displays that tell the story of the ferry service and rum-running.

Accommodations
Meadow Lodge Motel (Hwy. 1, 2 km west of the ferry, 902/962-2022 or 800/461-2022; mid-May-Sept.; $75-90 s or d) is a convenient accommodation if you're leaving the island early or arriving late.

Getting There
CAR
Wood Islands is about 35 kilometers (30 minutes) south of Orwell and 60 kilometers (one hour) southeast of Charlottetown via Route 1.

FERRY
Between May and mid-December (the rest of the year, ice in Northumberland Strait restricts shipping), ferries depart Wood Islands 5-9 times daily for Caribou, Nova Scotia. The crossing takes 75 minutes, but expect to wait at least that long during peak travel periods (July and August weekends). The round-trip fare is $69 per vehicle, including passengers. For a schedule, contact Northumberland Ferries (902/566-3838 or 877/635-7245, www.ferries.ca).

WOOD ISLANDS TO MURRAY HARBOUR
From Wood Islands, Route 4 continues into Kings County, making a sharp left inland to Murray River. Route 18 sticks to the coast, wrapping around Murray Head before leading into the town of Murray Harbour and then into Murray River.

Northumberland Provincial Park
Just three kilometers from Wood Islands, Northumberland Provincial Park (Rte. 4, 902/962-7418; late June-late Aug.) fronts the ocean, near enough to the terminal to see the ferries coming and going to Caribou. The park offers rental bikes, hayrides, a nature trail, a stream for fishing, an ocean beach with clam digging, and mini-golf. Facilities at the well-equipped campground include 60 sites (tent sites $28, hookups $32-35), a launderette, kitchen shelters, a nearby campers' store, and hot showers.

★ Rossignol Estate Winery
Beyond Northumberland Provincial Park, the highway crosses into Kings County and quickly reaches Prince Edward Island's only commercial winery, Rossignol Estate Winery (11147 Shore Rd., 902/962-4193, www.rossignolwinery.com; May-Oct. Mon.-Sat. 10am-5pm, Sun. noon-5pm, tastings free). Try not to let the glorious ocean

Rossignol Estate Winery

views distract you from the task at hand—tasting a wide range of reds and whites (including chardonnay and pinot cabernet), along with fruit wines and deliciously sweet blackberry mead. The winery produces 45,000 bottles annually and does everything right, including using oak barrels for aging. No tours are offered, but you are free to wander down the red dirt path leading to the ocean cliffs.

Murray Harbour to Souris

From Wood Islands, you'll pass through tiny hamlets like Little Sands and White Sands, marked more by road signs than clusters of houses as Route 18 approaches Murray Harbour. An enormous number of seals live in this well-sheltered harbor, and they love to loll about on offshore islands.

The Murray family settled the area and has namesakes everywhere: The Murray River flows into Murray Harbour, whose entrance is marked by Murray Head; seal colonies cluster on the harbor's Murray Islands; and the three seaport villages are Murray Harbour, Murray River, and Murray Harbour North.

MURRAY HARBOUR

On the south side of the bay is the small village of Murray Harbour. Beyond town to the east is **Beach Point Lighthouse,** from where seals are often visible.

Set on a five-hectare property, ★ **Fox River Cottages** (239 Machon Point Rd., 902/962-2881, www.foxriver.ca; May-early Oct.; $130-145 s or d) offers four two-bedroom housekeeping cottages with screened porches overlooking the Fox River. Amenities include a canoe, a rowboat, and laundry. Also in the area, **Harbour Motel** (174 Mill Rd., 902/962-3660; $90 s or d) has seven kitchen-equipped units within walking distance of town.

Easily the best place to eat in town, **Brehauts Restaurant** (7 Mariners Ln., 902/962-3141; Apr.-late Sept. Mon.-Sat. 8am-8pm, Sun. 11am-8pm; $11-18) has a big deck overlooking the river. The menu is strong on seafood, simply prepared and well priced.

Getting There

To get to Murray Harbour from Wood Islands, take Route 4 east then Route 18A north for 20 kilometers (20 minutes). From Charlottetown, take Route 1 west to Wood Islands, for a total distance of 80 kilometers (1.5 hours).

MURRAY RIVER

The oval-shaped harbor is centered on the town of Murray River, hub of the island's southeast corner.

Sights and Recreation

Children will love **King's Castle Provincial Park** (1887 Gladstone Rd., 902/962-7422; mid-June-mid-Sept. daily 9am-9pm; free) on the banks of the Murray River east of town. A grassy meadow is filled with concrete storybook characters, trails lead through the woods, and there's a riverside beach (complete with hot showers). A covered picnic shelter is the perfect spot for lunch.

If you like woodland walking, stretch your legs at **Murray River Pines,** a provincial woodlot near town. The site, off Route 4, is remote. Look for an abandoned mill, the former provincial Northumberland Mill and Museum, now closed; the woodlot is inland behind the site. A 30-minute hike on the red-clay road leads to dense groves of red and white pines, abutted by stands of balsam, red maple, and red spruce. The largest pines date to the 1870s, when England's Royal Navy cut down most of the forest for masts. Somehow these trees survived, and they have become havens for birds of all kinds, including blue herons, kingfishers, swallows, blue jays, and chickadees.

The **Old General Store** (9387 Main St., 902/962-2459; July-Aug. Mon.-Sat.

9:30am-5:30pm, Sun. noon-5pm; shorter hours in spring and fall) ranks as one of the island's best crafts sources, and stocks folk art, linens, and domestic wares.

Accommodations and Camping

On a small lake east of town, **Forest and Stream Cottages** (446 Fox River Rd., 902/962-3537 or 800/227-9943, www.forestandstreamcottages.com; mid-June-Oct.; $105-115 s or d) comprises six simple but tidy cottages, each with a kitchen, a bedroom, and a covered porch. Rowboats are supplied, and there's a playground.

Continue through town to the northeast to reach ★ **Seal Cove Campground** (87 Mink River Rd., 902/962-2745, www.sealcovecampground.ca; mid-May-Sept.; $23-42), which overlooks offshore seal colonies. When you're done watching seals, there's a nine-hole golf course ($22 greens fee for a full day), an outdoor pool, kayak rentals, and a playground to keep everyone busy.

Getting There

Murray River is 10 kilometers northwest of Murray Harbour via Route 18. From Charlottetown, take Route 1 west to Wood Islands and then Route 4 east and north, for a total of 80 kilometers (1.5 hours).

MURRAY RIVER TO MONTAGUE

Route 4 is the most direct road between Murray River and Montague, but Route 17 is more scenic.

Through the village of Murray Harbour North, **Poverty Beach,** at the end of a spur off Route 17, is a long narrow sandbar that separates the sea from the harbor. It's quiet, remote, and wrapped in a sense of primeval peacefulness. The peninsula is worth a trek, but think twice about swimming in the surf; powerful sea currents here can be dangerous, and no lifeguards are around to rescue foundering bathers.

Panmure Island

Panmure Island, a remote and windswept wilderness, lies 15 kilometers north of Poverty Beach. It is linked to the mainland by a narrow strip of land, traversed by Route 347, which rambles out along the flag-shaped peninsula that wags between St. Mary's Bay, Georgetown Harbour, and the sea. A supervised beach fronts the strait, and a wisp of a road angles into the interior and emerges at the waterfront with views of Georgetown across the harbor. Back on the mainland is **Panmure Island Provincial Park** (902/838-0668; late June-early Sept.). A campground here has 22 unserviced sites and 16 two-way hookup sites ($22-28), supervised ocean swimming off a beautiful white-sand beach, a launderette, a campers' canteen, fireplaces, and hot showers.

GETTING THERE

Via Route 17, Panmure Island is about 25 kilometers (25 minutes) north of Murray River. To get there from Charlottetown, take Route 1 west to Wood Islands, then Route 4 east and north, then Route 17 east and north, then Route 347 north, for a total of 105 kilometers (1.5 hours).

Buffalo Park

Halfway between Murray River and Montague along Route 4, the 40-hectare **Buffalo Provincial Park** (year-round; free) may seem deserted at first glance. If you look closely, though, you'll spot bison and white-tailed deer roaming the woodlands. The namesake herd began with 14 bison imported from Alberta in 1970 as part of a federal experiment to help preserve the almost-extinct species. There's still no population explosion, but the herd numbers around 25 buffalo now. No guarantees, but in mid-afternoon the bison herd often emerges to feed near the Route 4 fence.

MONTAGUE

Montague, 46 kilometers east of Charlottetown and 25 kilometers north of Wood Islands, is the largest town in Kings County, yet the population is under 2,000. The town is defined by the Main Street bridge over the Montague River. In fact, the town began as Montague Bridge in 1825, when the bridge was made of logs and the area had just four farms. Shipbuilding brought riches to the town, and many a schooner or other sailing craft was launched here on the broad river.

The town is uncomplicated, pretty, clean, and friendly. Everything important lies along Main Street, which slices through town and proceeds up, over, and down the bridge.

Sights and Recreation

GARDEN OF THE GULF MUSEUM

The **Garden of the Gulf Museum** (564 Main St., 902/838-2467; June-late Sept. Mon.-Sat. 9am-5pm; adult $5, cash only) is housed in an old post office overlooking Montague River at the bridge. The building is an impressive hulk of red brick with a steeply pitched roof, showing its French architectural influence. The collection includes exhibits on local history, including the colorful story of Trois Rivières, which was established nearby in 1732 by French entrepreneur Jean Pierre de Roma.

★ SEAL-WATCHING

Tightline Tours (1 Station St., 902/969-0412; adult $50, child $35) offers two-hour seal watching tours from the town's marina just off Route 4. Departure times are tide-dependent (so call ahead), but typically head downstream toward the ocean. The experienced captain knows the most likely places harbor seals will be sunning themselves along the shoreline, but you may also see them swimming near the boat. Birdlife includes great blue herons, gulls, and ospreys. On the return journey, freshly harvested mussels are boiled up on board for a memorable feast.

Accommodations

Overlooking the water, **Lanes Riverhouse Inn** (33 Brook St., 902/838-2433 or 800/268-7532, www.lanesriverhouseinn.com; $89-125

Harbour seals are often sighted on boat tours from Montague.

s or d) combines a newer 30-bedroom hotel with a pleasant cluster of older cottages that have basic cooking facilities. The hotel rooms are spacious and have river-facing balconies, air-conditioning, and the most comfortable beds in this part of the province.

Getting There

Via Route 315, Montague is 25 kilometers (25 minutes) north of Wood Islands. Via Routes 1 and 3, Montague is 45 kilometers (50 minutes) east of Charlottetown.

VICINITY OF MONTAGUE
Brudenell River
Provincial Park

The 30-hectare park-cum-resort called **Brudenell River Provincial Park** occupies a gorgeous pastoral setting on the peninsula that juts out into Cardigan Bay between the Brudenell and Cardigan Rivers. You enter the park from Route 3, five kilometers north of Montague and then three kilometers east of Pooles Corner, and the road winds through manicured grounds to Brundenell River Resort.

RECREATION

Golfers enjoy walking the fairways of two golf courses, **Brudenell River** and the newer **Dundarave** (902/652-8965 or 800/377-8336; May-Oct.; greens fees $80-90), which plays to a challenging 7,300 yards from the back tees. The courses both rank among Atlantic Canada's superior golf greens and have been the site of various national and Canadian Professional Golfers' Association tournaments.

Other park activities include canoeing (rentals $35 a day), windsurfing ($45 for a partial day), horseback riding (902/652-2396; $35 for a one-hour beach ride), indoor and outdoor pools, tennis, and boat tours. All park activities are open to campers, resort guests, and day visitors alike.

ACCOMMODATIONS AND FOOD

The epicenter of the resort complex is **Rodd Brudenell River** (902/652-2332 or 800/565-7633, www.roddhotelsandresorts.com; May-mid-Oct.; $180-280 s or d). Dating from the early 1990s, the resort holds two distinct types of rooms: contemporary and spacious hotel rooms in the main lodge and two-bedroom Echelon Gold Cottages, with kitchens and fireplaces. Check the website for deals and packages. The resort's riverfront **Gordon on the River** dining room is casually upscale and specializes in seafood entrées ($19-33); try the haddock stuffed with spinach and Italian Bocconcini cheese, and, for dessert, shortbread squares topped with lemon meringue or the homemade parfait.

The 15 modern units at ★ **Brudenell Chalets** (Rte. 3, 902/652-2900 or 866/652-2900, www.brudenellchalets.com; $225-350 s or d) are more like mini houses than chalets. Each has two to four bedrooms, a well-designed kitchen, a lounge with TV, washing and drying facilities, and a deck with a barbecue. On the edge of the park, the place is close to the golf course and also has its own outdoor swimming pool and playground.

CAMPING

The park isn't all resort. Continue beyond the main entrance to reach **Brudenell River Provincial Park Campground** (902/652-8966; mid-May-late Sept.). Tent sites are spread through a wooded area ($26), while hookup sites ($28-32) have plenty of room to maneuver big rigs. Amenities include hot showers, kitchen shelters, a launderette, interpretive programs, a riverfront beach, and a walking trail that links the campground to the resort.

Georgetown

Located at the end of Route 3, beyond Brudenell River Provincial Park, Georgetown was once a major shipbuilding center. The naming of Georgetown was surveyor Samuel Holland's tribute to George III of England. The port boasted one of the island's most perfectly created deepwater harbors. Its early economy was built with British money, however, and when England's economy had a short-lived collapse, Georgetown lost its economic edge and never regained it. Georgetown slid into the shadows, replaced by Montague

first as a shipbuilding and shipping center and then as the area's principal market town. It is now best known for the **King's Playhouse** (65 Grafton St., 902/652-2053, www.kingsplayhouse.com; June-mid-Sept.; $12-18), a repertory company that stages dramas and comedies in a downtown theater year-round.

Cardigan

At the hamlet of Cardigan, five kilometers north of Brudenell Provincial Park, **Cardigan Lobster Suppers** (4557 Wharf Rd., 902/583-2020; late June-early Oct. daily 5pm-9pm) are well worth partaking in. Seating is inside or outside, on a deck with sweeping water views. The full lobster supper is $39 per person (including all-you-can-eat seafood chowder), or there's a smaller version, with a smaller lobster, for $20 that is aimed at seniors and children.

BAY FORTUNE

About 30 kilometers northeast of Cardigan, Fortune River flows into Bay Fortune, which was named long before the fortunes of Broadway fueled the local retreats of producer David Belasco and playwright Elmer Harris. Upriver six kilometers is the hamlet of Dingwells Mills, where *Johnny Belinda,* one of Harris's most successful Broadway plays and later a movie, was set.

Accommodations and Food

The ★ **Inn at Bay Fortune** (Rte. 310, 902/687-3745, www.innatbayfortune.com; late May-mid-Oct.; $150-335 s or d) has earned an international reputation, thanks to the care lavished on the property by innkeeper David Wilmer. The estate was once the summer home of renowned playwright Elmer Harris, who designed the 19th-century version of a motel to house the entourage of thespians who traveled with him. The 17 guest rooms (14 with fireplaces) are impeccably furnished and filled with natural light. The most sought-after is the two-level Tower Suite, which has sweeping water views from the upstairs lounge. Rates include a cooked breakfast.

A strong sense of conviviality pervades the inn's dining room, which is regarded as one of Canada's finest restaurants. Meals are served on the front enclosed porch during summer or inside with tables arranged before the fireplace when the weather is cooler. The creative menu features entrées emphasizing local products from both the land and the sea (try scallops topped with strawberry and balsamic salsa), accompanied by a sophisticated wine list. Although you don't need to be a guest to dine here, many are, staying as part of a package.

Getting There

Bay Fortune is 30 kilometers (30 minutes) north of Cardigan via Routes 4 and 332. To get there from Charlottetown, head west on Routes 1, 3, 4, and 332 for 70 kilometers (1.5 hours).

Souris and Vicinity

Any islander will tell you that the fishing town of Souris is "far out," the end of the line on the beaten tourist track. The town (pop. 1,200), notched on the strait seacoast 80 kilometers east of Charlottetown and 45 kilometers north of Montague, garners unqualified raves for its setting. Consider Souris as a base for touring throughout the northeast. The location translates as good value for the dollar in lodgings and dining. The restaurants are plainly furnished and specialize in seafood platters, ranked by islanders among the province's best and freshest.

SIGHTS AND RECREATION

The town overlooks Northumberland Strait from sloping headlands, bounded in part by grasslands that sweep down to the water and in other parts by steeply pitched red cliffs. On the southern boundary, the Souris River rushes toward the sea in a gush of red water and pours into the blue strait, like a palette of blended watercolor pigments.

Townshend Woodlot

Townshend Woodlot is a 106-hectare spread that closely resembles the island's original Acadian forest. In 1970, the International Biological Program designated the setting as one of the island's finest examples of old-growth hardwood groves. To get there, take Route 305 three kilometers north to the hamlet of Souris Line Road. The woodlot plantation lies off the road, fairly well hidden and obscurely marked—you may want to ask for directions in Souris. Acquired by the province in 1978, the woodlot lacks a clear hiking route, but it's easily walkable on a level grade of sandy loam. The groves meld beech trees—a species that once dominated half the

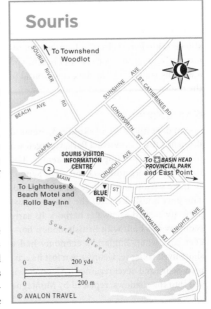

Souris

island's forests—with yellow birch, red maple, and sugar maple, whose dark brown trunks stretch up as high as 32 meters. Eastern chipmunks nest in underground tunnels. Dwarf ginseng—rare on the island—and nodding trillium thrive.

★ Basin Head Provincial Park

Formed by the winds, most sand dunes grow and creep along, albeit at a snail's pace. At Basin Head Provincial Park, off Route 16, 13 kilometers east of Souris, the dunes are known as "walking" dunes for their wind-blown mobility. The high silica content of the sand here and at nearby Red Point Provincial Park causes it to squeak audibly when crunched underfoot; islanders poetically describe the phenomenon as "singing sands." At Basin Head, the dunes are high and environmentally fragile; visitors should stay off the dunes and tread instead along the beach near the water's edge. But the beach is most popular simply for being somewhere to sunbathe and swim throughout summer, and it can get very busy.

Access to the beach is from the end of Basin Head Road, which is also home to the Basin Head Fisheries Museum (Rte. 16, 902/357-7233; mid-June-late Sept. daily 9am-5pm; adult $4, child $3.50), which sits high on the headland overlooking the beach and an inlet you must cross to reach the sand. Here you'll find boats, nets, and a museum with expertly conceived exhibits detailing the historic inshore fishing industry and local coastal ecology.

FESTIVALS AND EVENTS

In early July, musicians from across the island and beyond gather southeast of town at Rollo Bay for the Prince Edward Island Bluegrass & Old Time Music Festival (www.bluegrasspei.com), where a weekend ticket costs $45. The highlight of the local event calendar is the late-July Mermaid Tears Sea Glass Festival (www.peiseaglassfestival.com), which, as the name suggests, features sea glass art in a variety of forms, as well as family-friendly events through the town.

ACCOMMODATIONS AND CAMPING

Fronting the ocean and within walking distance of a beach, Lighthouse and Beach Motel (51 Sheep Pond Rd., off Rte. 2, 902/687-2339 or 800/689-2339, www.

The beach at Basin Head is famous for its "singing sands."

lighthouseandbeachmotel.ca; mid-June-mid-Sept.; $80-100 s or d) offers regular motel rooms with a light breakfast included in the rates. An old lighthouse on the property is rented by the week ($700) and has a jetted tub, separate bedrooms, and a kitchen. This lodging is two kilometers west of town.

A further six kilometers west is **Rollo Bay Inn** (Rte. 2, 902/687-3550 or 877/687-3550; $99 s or d). This lodging combines a re-created Georgian setting with 15 rooms, housekeeping units, and suites on spacious grounds with a restaurant serving basic island cuisine.

Red Point Provincial Park (13 km east of Souris, off Rte. 16, 902/357-2463; late June-early Sept.) has a campground with 32 tent sites ($22) and 58 powered sites ($28). Amenities include kitchen shelters, fireplaces, and hot showers.

FOOD

The ★ **Blue Fin** (10 Federal Ave., 902/687-3271; daily 8am-8pm; $9-18) is partly protected from the tourist crowd by its tucked-away location off the main street. But for well-priced simple seafood dishes, it's well worth searching out. The seafood chowder and the fish-and-chips are both excellent.

INFORMATION

Souris Visitor Information Centre (95 Main St., 902/687-7030; mid-June-mid-Oct. daily 9am-5pm) is in a historic building in the middle of town.

GETTING THERE

Souris is 45 kilometers (40 minutes) northeast of Montague via Route 4 and Route 2. From Charlottetown, it's an 80-kilometer (1.5-hour) drive northeast to Souris along Route 5, Route 4, then Route 2.

North Shore

If you like photogenic landscapes, windy seacoasts washed with tossing surf, and weathered seaports, consider northeastern Kings County for a revealing glimpse of this seafaring island as it once was. Beyond Souris, the strait seacoast stretches 25 kilometers to windswept East Point, the island's easternmost point. On the equally remote gulf coast in this region, you'll find few tourists, a dozen tiny seaports, and a handful of lonesome lighthouses that stand as sentinels along the 75-kilometer-long coastline, strewn with centuries of shipwrecks.

FAR EAST
East Point

At the northeastern tip of Prince Edward Island, 25 kilometers northeast of Souris, Northumberland Strait and the Gulf of St. Lawrence meet in a lathered flush of cresting seas, sometimes colored blue and often tinged with red from oxide-colored silt. Here

stands the 20-meter-high octagonal tower of **East Point Lighthouse** (404 Lighthouse Rd., off Rte. 16, 902/357-2106; mid-June-early Sept. daily 9am-6pm; guided tours adult $3, senior $2, child $1), which is still in use. The first lighthouse at this spot was built in 1867, but erosion has forced subsequent structures to be moved farther back from the cliff edge.

GETTING THERE

East Point is 100 kilometers (two hours) northeast of Charlottetown via Route 5, Route 4, Route 2, then Route 16. From Souris, it's about 25 kilometers (25 minutes) north on Route 16 to East Point.

Elmira

Elmira Railway Museum (Rte. 16A, 902/357-7234; June-late Sept. daily 9am-5pm; adult $4) is the end of the line—literally. This is where a rail line that once spanned Prince Edward Island came to an end. The original station now serves as a testament to the island railroad's halcyon years, with the province's only exhibits and documentation on rail service. The museum is on the Confederation Trail, the old rail bed, which has been converted to a walking and bike path that extends 279 kilometers to the west end of the island.

GETTING THERE

Elmira is about 20 kilometers (20 minutes) north of Souris just off of Route 16. From Charlottetown, it's about 95 kilometers (1.5 hours) via Souris on Routes 5, 4, 2, then 16.

North Lake and Vicinity

North Lake harbor is one of four departure points for deep-sea fishing; anglers try for trophy catches of giant bluefin tuna, which can grow to 500 kilograms (1,000 pounds). Expect to pay up to $1,250 for a full-day charter for up to six anglers. Trips depart daily during the July to early October season from North Lake, Naufrage, Launching, and Red Head harbors. Tony's Tuna Fishing (902/357-2055, www. tonystunafishing.com), at North Lake harbor, is among the most respected operators.

Points East Beach Motel (7 Cape Rd., 902/357-2228, www.peimotel.com; July-Sept.; $115-140 s or d) has 10 above-average motel rooms right on the beach.

Campbells Cove Campground (Rte. 16, 3 km west of North Lake, 902/357-3080, www.campbellscovecampground.com; late June-early Sept.; campsites $26-32, cabins $52-86 s or d) fronts the gulf and a long stretch of beautiful sandy beach that is rarely crowded. In addition to campsites and basic cabins, facilities include kitchen shelters, a Laundromat, and a convenience store.

GETTING THERE

North Lake is about eight kilometers (10 minutes) west of East Point via Route 16. It's about 100 kilometers (1.5 hours) to get to North Lake via the northern route (east on Route 2 and Route 16) from Charlottetown. Or use the southern route (east on Route 5, Route 4, Route 2, then Route 16), also 100

kilometers, but a slightly longer driving time (1.5 hours).

GULF SHORE
St. Peters Bay

If you're in the area the first week of August, check out the port's Wild Blueberry Festival (www.stpetersblueberryfestival. com), an islander favorite with concerts, entertainment, blueberry dishes, lobster and beef barbecue, and a pancake brunch.

At St. Peters Campground (5930 St. Peters Rd., 902/961-2786; mid-June-Sept.; $25-32 per night), you have a choice of 11 unserviced sites and more than 70 full-hookup sites. Amenities include a launderette, kitchen shelters, free firewood, two swimming pools, mini-golf, and hot showers.

GETTING THERE

St. Peters Bay is about 30 kilometers (25 minutes) northwest of Souris via Route 2. It's 50 kilometers (50 minutes) northeast of Charlottetown, also on Route 2.

★ Prince Edward Island National Park, Greenwich Unit

Take Route 313 west from St. Peters along the north side of St. Peters Bay to reach the easternmost of three units that comprise Price Edward Island National Park. Known as the Greenwich Unit, this six-square-kilometer tract of land encompasses a fragile dune system and wetlands. Near the end of the park access road is Greenwich Interpretation Centre (902/963-2391; mid-June-mid-Sept. 10am-4pm, until 6pm in July and Aug.). Admission to the park is adult $8, senior $7, child $4. From the interpretive center, a boardwalk leads across the dunes to the beach, but the hiking trails starting from the very end of the road are the highlight. The 4.8-kilometer (round-trip) Greenwich Dunes Trail, which leads through a coastal forest and across the dunes, typifies the coastal habitat best. Wind is slowly pushing the dunes here back into the forest, burying trees that over time become bleached skeletons—an intriguing and unique sight.

MORELL AND VICINITY

Berries are the focus at Morell, 40 minutes from Charlottetown. The St. Peters Bay seaport makes much of the harvest at mid-July's six-day **Morell River Run Festival,** with a parade, concerts, dances, barbecues, strawberry desserts, and other community events.

★ Crowbush Cove

Along the coast just west of Morell is the **Links at Crowbush Cove** (902/368-5761; May-Oct.), a highly acclaimed, 18-hole, par-73 golf course. A links course in the Scottish tradition, Crowbush challenges players with nine water holes and nine holes surrounded by dunes. Greens fees are $90-110. Overlooking the golf course is ★ **Rodd Crowbush Golf & Beach Resort** (902/961-5600, www.rodd-vacations.com; mid-May-mid-Oct.), comprising contemporary rooms in the main lodge and two-bedroom cottages spread along the course. Amenities include spa services, a fitness center, an indoor pool, tennis courts, and

a restaurant overlooking the course. Most guests stay as part of golf packages, from $230 per person per night.

Getting There

Morell is about 40 kilometers (40 minutes) west of Souris via Route 2, and about 40 kilometers (40-minute drive) northeast of Charlottetown via Route 2.

MOUNT STEWART

Located on the Hillsborough River, 30 kilometers northeast of Charlottetown, Mount Stewart grew as a shipbuilding center in the second half of the 19th century. Today, instead of shipyards, the draw is the **Confederation Trail,** a rail bed that has been converted to a hiking and biking trail that spans the entire island. Mount Stewart is a good place to base yourself for a day or overnight trip along a short section of the trail.

The main attraction in town is the **Hillsborough River Eco-Centre** (104 Main St., 902/676-2050; July-Aug. daily 10am-6pm; free), which has displays on the river and its ecosystem, public Internet access, and a gift

a deserted beach in the Greenwich Unit of Prince Edward Island National Park

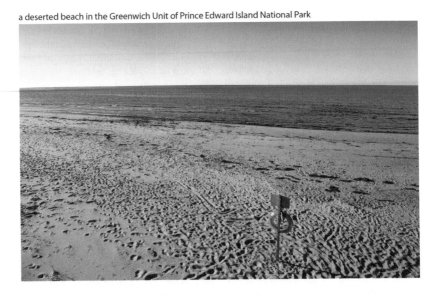

Ferries to Îles de la Madeleine

Souris is the departure point for ferries to Québec's Îles de la Madeleine (Magdalen Islands), in the Gulf of St. Lawrence, 105 kilometers from the northern tip of Prince Edward Island and 215 kilometers from the closest point of Québec. This remote archipelago comprises 12 islands, 6 of which are linked by rolling sand dunes, and totals 200 square kilometers. The islands are renowned as a remote wilderness destination, featuring great beaches and abundant bird life. Villages dot the islands, and each has basic tourist services.

CTMA Ferry (418/986-3278 or 888/986-3278, www.ctmatraversier.ca/en) operates a vehicle/passenger ferry between Souris and the islands year-round. The 134-kilometer crossing takes five hours, with a schedule that includes 6-8 sailings weekly in each direction. Most runs leave Souris at 2pm and leave Cap-aux-Meules for the return at 8am. One-way passenger fares are adult $50, senior $40, child $29, vehicle from $93.

For information on the Magdalens, contact the local **tourism office** (128 Chemin Débarcadère, Cap-aux-Meules, 418/986-2245). This office also maintains an excellent website, www.ilesdelamadeleine.com, with detailed island information and links to accommodations.

shop. Make sure to climb the tower out back for sweeping views up and down Prince Edward Island's major river.

The ★ **Trailside Café & Inn** (109 Main St., 902/394-3626, www.trailside.ca; April-Nov.; $89 s or d) is named for the Confederation Trail, which passes through town. Located in a restored general store, the four rooms each have private bathrooms, hardwood floors, and televisions. For those looking at traveling the trail, this is a handy place to rent bikes ($25 the first day, $10 per additional day). The in-house café serves up a limited but varied menu of local specialties, all for under $15. The Trailside often hosts local musicians, including every Sunday at 11am through summer, when brunch and live music costs just $19 per person.

Getting There

Mount Stewart is on Route 2, 15 kilometers (10 minutes) southeast of Morell and 30 kilometers (35 minutes) northeast of Charlottetown.

Photo Credits

MAP SYMBOLS

▦ Expressway	○ City/Town	✈ Airport	⚲ Golf Course
Primary Road	◉ State Capital	✖ Airfield	🅿 Parking Area
Secondary Road	✳ National Capital	▲ Mountain	⬟ Archaeological Site
Unpaved Road	★ Point of Interest	✛ Unique Natural Feature	▮ Church
Feature Trail	• Accommodation		⛽ Gas Station
Other Trail	▼ Restaurant/Bar	Waterfall	Glacier
Ferry		▲ Park	Mangrove
Pedestrian Walkway	■ Other Location	⬛ Trailhead	Reef
Stairs	⋀ Campground	⛷ Skiing Area	Swamp

CONVERSION TABLES

°C = (°F - 32) / 1.8
°F = (°C x 1.8) + 32
1 inch = 2.54 centimeters (cm)
1 foot = 0.304 meters (m)
1 yard = 0.914 meters
1 mile = 1.6093 kilometers (km)
1 km = 0.6214 miles
1 fathom = 1.8288 m
1 chain = 20.1168 m
1 furlong = 201.168 m
1 acre = 0.4047 hectares
1 sq km = 100 hectares
1 sq mile = 2.59 square km
1 ounce = 28.35 grams
1 pound = 0.4536 kilograms
1 short ton = 0.90718 metric ton
1 short ton = 2,000 pounds
1 long ton = 1.016 metric tons
1 long ton = 2,240 pounds
1 metric ton = 1,000 kilograms
1 quart = 0.94635 liters
1 US gallon = 3.7854 liters
1 Imperial gallon = 4.5459 liters
1 nautical mile = 1.852 km

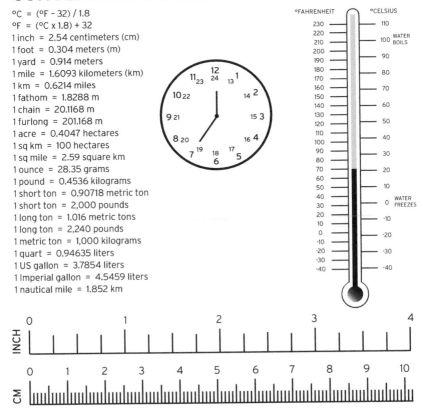

MOON SPOTLIGHT
PRINCE EDWARD ISLAND
Avalon Travel
a member of the Perseus Books Group
1700 Fourth Street
Berkeley, CA 94710, USA
www.moon.com

Editor: Leah Gordon
Series Manager: Kathryn Ettinger
Copy Editor: Kristie Reilly
Graphics Coordinators: Kathryn Osgood,
 Elizabeth Jang
Production Coordinator: Elizabeth Jang
Cover Design: Faceout Studios, Charles Brock
Moon Logo: Tim McGrath
Map Editor: Kat Bennett
Cartographers: Brian Shotwell, Stephanie Poulain

ISBN-13: 978-1-63121-096-9

Front cover photo: Panmure Island lighthouse in the
Atlantic shore of Prince Edward Island © Gvictoria |
Dreamstime.com

Printed in the United States

All recommendations, including those for sights,
activities, hotels, restaurants, and shops, are based
on each author's individual judgment. We do not
accept payment for inclusion in our travel guides,
and our authors don't accept free goods or services
in exchange for positive coverage.

Although every effort was made to ensure that
the information was correct at the time of going
to press, the author and publisher do not assume
and hereby disclaim any liability to any party for any
loss or damage caused by errors, omissions, or any
potential travel disruption due to labor or financial
difficulty, whether such errors or omissions result
from negligence, accident, or any other cause.

About the Author

Andrew Hempstead

© DIANNE MELTON

As a professional travel writer, Andrew spends as much time as possible out on the road. During his travels, he experiences the many and varied delights of Prince Edward Island the same way his readers do.

Since the early 1990s, Andrew has authored and updated more than 60 guidebooks, and supplied content for regional and national clients like Expedia and KLM. His photography has appeared in a wide variety of media, ranging from international golf magazines to a Ripley's Believe it or Not! Museum.

Andrew and his wife Dianne own Summerthought Publishing, a Canadian regional publisher of nonfiction books. He is a member of The Diners Club® World's 50 Best Restaurants Academy. Andrew has also spoken on travel writing to a national audience and has contributed to a university-level travel writing textbook.

CPSIA information can be obtained at www.ICGtesting.com
Printed in the USA
LVOW01s0915220415

435461LV00001B/1/P